NOT ME

MARIANNE DISSARD is a singer, performer, lyricist and filmmaker from Tucson, Arizona. Born in the French Pyrénées, she now splits her time between her wooden boat Wendy Woo in the English harbour of Ramsgate and a stone shack near Matera, Italy. Her cat, Edith, lives with her parents. *Not Me* is her first book.

PRAISE FOR *NOT ME*

"Marianne Dissard writes beautifully, finding poetry even in the bleakest experiences, elevating and illuminating both in the process. This book reminded me a little of Burroughs, a little more of Knausgaard in its crack-like ability to make me want to pick it straight back up whenever I put it down. Often improbably funny, too, *Not Me* is without doubt one of the best books I've read this year."

Andrew Smith, *Moondust* and *Totally Wired*

"Marianne Dissard is that rare sort of talent: a literary chanteuse who renders the whole world with keen observations, wit, and pathos."

Mitch Cullin, *A Slight Trick of the Mind* and *Tideland*

"Not just painfully honest, but viscerally, brutally honest. Marianne Dissard's description of living with bulimia gives an uncomfortably physical riposte to the widely misheld idea that it is basically nipping off to the bathroom to throw up dessert. Lacking even the noxious fake glamour of anorexia, bulimia is exposed in all its controlling wretchedness as Dissard struggles with the condition, while at the same time managing independently to sustain an international career as a touring singer songwriter. This is not a manual for how to deal with bulimia—it is a struggle for survival, and ultimately self-acceptance."

John Parish, *Let England Shake* and *How Animals Move*

"Being given such stark access to someone's private world could be disturbing (it is), should be uncomfortable (it can be), but when the internal dialogue is as frank and compelling as Marianne's, the overarching emotion it elicits is compassion. There's humour too, it's just dark…from banquets for one in a Parisian apartment to almost thriller like gastronomic chases through the backstreets of Palermo seeking fulfillment or a desire ultimately for nothingness…this is one very human story."

Shaun Hendry, *Scaledown* and *Vacilando '68*

"Visceral, explosive and ultimately uplifting, Dissard's is a story of true strength of character—the refusal to give up and the realisation that sometimes that is exactly what is needed."

Megan Garrett-Jones, *Things With Words*

"My overwhelming feeling was of reading something that I shouldn't be reading. Like stumbling across someone's secret diary at the bottom of a drawer. It isn't the sort of memoir that's designed to come across as 'raw' and 'honest' in a way that makes the writer look cool, it's actually genuinely honest to a degree that few people ever achieve even when writing purely for themselves. It's also refreshingly free of attempts to explain and justify and conceptualise, which only heightens the thrill of being privy to someone's private rather than public thoughts."

Raphael Mann

"The concordant celebration of food and sound was my first occasion to share a stage, and a meal, with Marianne Dissard. We performed at a now defunct Brooklyn establishment dedicated to offering immersive flights of new music and haute cuisine for an audience furtively outgrowing its punk-dive milieu. Marianne's elastically idiosyncratic verve as a performer and documentarian belies a struggle with otherness and existence that her new memoir Not Me explores with honesty, humor and insight. The corporeal and psychic demands of a peripatetic life, from childhood to burgeoning success, is a universal tale. Family, food and music. Purpose and self-worth. Neither victim nor heroine, Marianne's unfinished journey will leave you somewhat shocked, curious and resolutely hopeful."

Paul Wallfisch, *Stadttheater Dortmund* and *Botanica*

"An unflinching, lyrical, funny, unguarded translation of the subtext to orchestrating her public life as a performer, singer, songwriter, and yogini around her private world of bulimia. Marianne does not gently lift the veil, she pulls the whole contraption down that held it up for so many years to reveal, intimately, the weight of keeping her secret a secret. A fantastic and ultimately inspiring read."

Vicki Brown, *Winter Garden* and *Sea And Trees*

ALSO BY MARIANNE DISSARD

Studio albums

The Cat. Not Me (2014)
L'abandon (2011)
L'entredeux (2008)

City Series and other albums

Cibola Gold : Best Of 2008-2015 (2016)
Cologne Vier Takes (2015)
Berlin Two Takes (2012)
Paris One Takes (2011)
Dedicated To Your Walls. May They Keep Blooming (2006)

Films

Lonesome Cowgirls (2010)
Low Y Cool (1996)
Drunken Bees (1995)
Post No Bills (1989)

Available on all streaming platforms.
Physical releases on Bandcamp, eBay and Amazon.
Films and music videos on YouTube, except Drunken Bees on eBay.

First published in 2019 by Marianne Dissard.

This is a work of nonfiction. Any similarity between the characters and situations within its pages, and places, persons, or animals living or dead, could be unintentional and co-incidental. Some names and identifying details have been changed or omitted to, in part, protect the privacy of individuals.

British Library Cataloguing in Publication Data.
A catalogue record for this book is available from the British Library.

ISBN: 978-1-9993131-0-4 (paperback)
ISBN: 978-1-9993131-1-1 (ebook)
ISBN: 978-1-9993131-2-8 (audiobook)

Typeset in Berling
Printed and bound by CPI in the UK.

Cover Design and typesetting by Jamie Keenan.
Cover photo by Flavien Prioreau.

mariannedissard.com
@mariannedissard

MARIANNE DISSARD

NOT ME

a memoir

To Edith

J'en ai fait, des hôtels et des caves.
J'en ai perdu du temps.
J'en ai fait des chiottes et des rades.
J'en ai bavé du sang.

— from *The Cat. Not Me.*

1

THE DRY AIR WHEEZES through my throat. I breathe through the mouth. I can't use my nose, the cavities inflamed or stuffed up, likely both. Reaching out for the bathroom sink with both hands, I pull myself up. My body tightens with pain, burned and bruised on the inside. Plaster loosening, the sink wobbles, its screws grabbing at dust. I make the same mental note I always do at this point: Get it fixed.

Good girl. Now file the note away. You won't act on it anyhow. What matters is you've made a note. Note for note, bonne note, always the A student. Pride, and maybe once the joy, but daddy's not around, there's no one around to keep track of the outcome. You can get away with murder.

Upright now and leaning into the mirror, I look for my face. It's all part of the ritual. I know what I'm looking for. I'm looking for confirmation from downturned lips that I'm less than shit. The sour pucker snicker that, really, I'm such a terrible choice for a human being and that, really, I'm not worthy of living. Not this life, not my life.

Nothing. I see nothing in the mirror. No mirror either. I'm facing the mirror—that, I know—but I can't see it, or myself in it. Right this second I can't see anything. Why didn't I notice it before getting up? Is it because I stood up too quickly and got lightheaded? There's a ringing in my ears, and a massive headache pounds the base of my skull. And now the view from my perch is set to bleak—black with streaks of mauve, or is it piss yellow? The color is indefinable. Why can't I tell? I focus, stare into the darkness and observe starry specks of white pixels in front of, inside of, my eyes. I've never seen these before. They burst and move with the languor of seaweeds flicked by a calm sea.

Light sputtering, it dawns on me that I may have done something irreversible. It excites me. It shakes me in the same way the smell of warm blood stirs the carnivorous hunter. The irreversible, the cold truth of permanence, and the end of the burden of choice—hair-raising shit—they animate me all. Could this be my luck? What was different today? Did I really make myself blind?

Think. You gotta cancel the show in Phoenix tomorrow. Must. You have to get out of it somehow. You must find an excuse. Say your Cadillac broke down, the old beast, stuck on an off-ramp in Eloy overnight. You've never cancelled a show before. Not this girl. But heed this blindness! It's a good enough reason to cancel. Right now, you can't even stand up straight. So? What if you did it anyway, what if you crawled onto that stage and sang your heart out like the butt-ugly blobfish that you are? Oh, wouldn't that be something? A blistering and unequivocal fuck you to bad luck. Ah, but my voice? Glazed by juices more acrid than turned wine, what sounds would this throat make, words boiled unintelligible from raspy syllables, a wheezing flow of tepid weakness disguised as demure coquetry. It doesn't fucking matter. You sing in French. They're Americans. Make sounds, any sounds. It all sounds the same, exotic and sexy, Parisian. Still, wouldn't someone notice you'd gone awry? They know you, some of them, and some of it. And the photos? You sure don't look like your press shots anymore. You look simply ravaged.

No one would care. They'd look through me on the fogged stage. Dear audience, you eat up the dream machine, don't you, and egg me on with your need to dream. Up there under the spotlights, a backlit midget like myself towers taller than a giraffe. Up there, stick figures a mere five feet away from you, we're fleshed out by a lot of junk thrown our way, puppets whose strings you, dear good audience, will pull and snap along to the music. Just do it, girl. Get on that stage. But is it a private drama or a staged performance, and couldn't it be both? The entrance fee is fair. Give what you can and buckle up tight. You know you want it too.

Yes, tonight, in my bathroom in Tucson, Arizona, in the winter of 2013, digging into the wound excites me so much that I'm scared. At last, scared of myself! I imagine it is something like pulling the trigger at Russian roulette once, twice, as many times as can be forgotten and they're all blanks and it doesn't matter but for the juice of adrenaline and the intoxicating smell of the powder. And then one day at last, it's a live bullet and that's really, really thrilling and you want to do it again because you like feeling the hardness of the truth but you're dead; you just died and it's too late, you're not around to tell the truth. Couldn't anyone tell you it always ends that way?

Warmth, a softness. I feel something, a silky coat, brushing along my calves. Cat. I kneel on the cold tiles, my back to the toilet bowl, hands reaching out to grab and pull Cat onto my lap. Chest tight, I try to breathe more deeply. We nuzzle. I am close to tears. In and out, full and empty. I try to think about breathing and just breathing. After some time, the ringing in my ears siphons away, my vision returns, and I begin to make out the rims of Cat's ears and inside them, a white fuzz, jumbled like the hair that sticks out from an old man's nostril. Stripes of gray and black fur come into focus around her eyes and I look into the slits, narrowing, of two huge, yellow-green irises. Cat, my Cat. My striped six-toed domestic shorthair American tabby Cat belts out her Yo! meow, in the way that roughly translates as "Yo, you! Feed me. Tis that time. All else will pass."

2

WE NEVER FOUGHT OVER her pâté, so I guess it didn't make much difference to her how fucked up I was. From the day I bought her—"cute tabby kitten," Craigslisted for twenty bucks—to the last, when I relinquished her, with visiting rights, in room-and-board care of my mother, we had six good years together. The day we met, sensing a disruption to her lifestyle, she had bolted up the stairs to hide under a bed and refused to cooperate until the brat who owned her yanked her out by the tail. Driving back together to my house, little could she know, hiding this time under the car seat, that this was only the first of our many planes, trains, and automobiles trips around the world. Although alike in our fear of dogs and loud noises, and dreading carbs and strangers both, we favored different havens when spooked—she'd shiver it off in a closet whereas I'd head straight for the bathroom. Only days after we became an item,

I had her spayed and remained childless myself in sympathy. More exactly, I was terrorized of giving birth, but I wasn't aware of it. I wasn't aware of much in those days. Cat took it all in stride. Together, we traipsed from America to Europe where my routine of dreadful deeds kept us homebound for a while. I listened to Cat and she stared back, her long silences heaping the understanding I craved. Meowing at each other, scratching and sniffing at the luggage I wouldn't put away. It was the best I could do under the circumstances.

3

SIX MONTHS LATER, I'M at the Palermo airport, heading from Sicily to Paris, where I'll be attending a four-week-long yoga intensive, a daily workshop that doubles as teacher certification training. It's something to try.

Incidentally, it's my birthday today. The hard-boiled eggs have whispered it to me. There are six of them tucked in my handbag, and although I've carefully managed to not think much about this day, this birth-day, the eggs have spoken. I'm forty-five.

Going through security, I take Cat out of her carrier and holding her tight, my thumb and index finger around her collar, I walk us through the portal. *Do not go on the lam, I plead.*

Today, I won't be celebrating my birthday. No party favors, no cake, no candles. Aside from the habitual, early-morning, one-liner email from my mother wishing me a good one, I don't expect anyone else to write or call to wish me a happy anything. Today, May 20th, 2013, I will be spending the day alone—with Cat—traveling, going places. I like that best. Being alone. Going places.

No wonder I took to the life of a touring musician. In 2006, for my first concert outside of Tucson, I skipped across the Arizona/New Mexico border, a six-hour drive for a house show in Albuquerque. In a living room cleared of furniture, I sang to a captive audience sitting in five neat rows and over those, out of reach, eyed the homemade cookies and bowls of guacamole, salsa, and chips on the kitchen counter of my potluck party. That night, fifty people drank my every breath and followed my every sway. I got hooked on strangers looking at me as if I was a blank slate. A beautiful, desirable, and clean slate.

When I asked my folks for help in fronting the cost of the yoga training, they said yes almost right away, relieved, I thought, that their one daughter might at last be wising up and settling on a real profession of the sort recognized by a paper certificate. I especially sensed my mother's gladness, successful as she had been in presenting the scheme to my father for approval. He owned the purse but she always held the strings. Over the past decade, they had watched me go through, in unorthodox order, a fast and painless divorce—a matter of bureaucracy—followed by a dragged-out separation from my musician husband. Being divorced didn't bring us closer together. At the same time, I was embarking on a singing career myself. If my ex-hubby could do it, I would show the world I could do it better than him—a turn of events I was, in retrospect, ill prepared to take on and recover from.

I'm moving back to Europe, I told my parents, and would settle in Palermo—a baffling choice, maybe, since Sicily was not a place where I had ever toured or consequently had any fans or music collaborators. Not to mention I didn't speak any Italian—or Sicilian, for that matter. But I felt strongly about living in a town whose boarded-up storefronts and unruly nightlife reminded me of the roaring Tucson of my twenties. Twenty years prior, Tucson had been my refuge from a workaholic lifestyle in Los Angeles. The AA town, I nicknamed it. Again I was moving to the closest thing to a remote desert island I could stand, a haven safe from family and distraction. In off-the-radar Sicily, I hoped, I would get myself back on my feet.

But there was one more thing I had to do before reclusing in Palermo. I was going to go through that yoga teacher workshop in Paris. My mother knew well that I had been a devoted yogini for over ten years now. She could see that yoga mattered, but didn't quite get why I kept touring and recording when it seemed like so much stress and cost me so much time and money. Although she never said it out loud, I'm convinced she must have thought it a great idea that I become a teacher. I wasn't about to disclose to her I had no intention of becoming one—that would have spoiled her fun, and mine. So I pretended this was something that mattered very much to me while both my parents pretended to believe me, and with that, the guilt on both sides was assuaged by a bit of action and a nice amount of money.

I wasn't moving back to Europe to be closer to them. Still healthy and remarkably self-managing in their early seventies, they didn't need taking care of, and I didn't like being close to them. It hadn't felt safe for many decades. For good and worse, money had long been at that time the only tender allowed in our relationship. They didn't even dare ask me anymore how

I was, how I felt, or if things were okay. Granted, when I told them I was getting married, I was only twenty-six, but my father's only utterance was to ask, unnerved and worried, if I was certain my soon-to-be wasn't marrying me for my money. He certainly meant his money, but I didn't even think to point that out to him.

So my mom sent a check to the yoga studio for my training, relieved to be of some use, maybe hoping I'd mellow out and give them some love in return. Thing is, I'd given up on that barter years ago and thought I'd stopped caring. I didn't realize how much I despised myself for asking them for help, nor did I know we'd been repeating that infernal transaction ever since I had become sick as a teenager. Family is a sticky thing. There's no soap, no acid strong enough to wash it off my bilious hands.

Six eggs, six hours. Earlier this morning in the kitchen of the apartment on Piazza Sant'Euno, I dropped six eggs from the diving board of a teaspoon into boiling water. With each drop, I mouthed the egg-an-hour mantra. I don't like wasting food. The plan was to be away from Palermo for at least a month and I wouldn't leave a morsel behind in the fridge. I maintain a tight kitchen, keep a clean house, and a waterproof schedule. Save for unopened cans of cat food, some olive oil, and concentrated lemon juice, the shelves have now been wiped out. The eggs, I told myself—no, I swore to myself—I'd eat one at a time at the top of each hour. No faster, no slower than that. Six eggs, the length of my trip from the ivory-cream bird nest over La Kalsa's most surreal piazza to Montmartre and my parents' parquetted two-bedroom apartment at the bottom northern flank of the posh Parisian hill.

It's hard to overdo it on boiled eggs. If I swallowed in a

single big gulp one whole shelled egg, and two or three or even four, I'd fast be gasping for air. Death by egg-choke. I don't want to go that way. No, I don't want to end up garroting eggs, suffocating in an airplane of all places. Yuk. I fear getting stuck more than anything. I'm the party guest who always knows which door to use to disappear without saying goodbye. Give me an escape route or give me death. I never know when I might turn into a werewolf.

At the gate, passengers are antsing to get in line and drop their suitcases along an imaginary meridian. I don't want to take my place quite yet. It's pointless, joining the ranks. We'll all get inside that plane and get to Paris at the same time. The prospect of sitting still for two hours and fifteen minutes weighing on my mind, I do want to make the effort to put in a few more steps and to keep aerating this aching body of mine. I walk toward the gate screen to look up the information, and amble on. Noted. This gate is where I must get back to eventually. Got it. I'm compassed now. I take a few more steps and expand the zone of comfort. With a few minutes to play at exploration and improvise myself—will myself—other than bored at the airport, I'm in charge. How about timing my expedition through the terminal so I'm last to get on the plane? Move! Be the smartest. Keep moving. Stay free. Balance cat-carrier on one arm. Flex these muscles. Burn energy. Keep the edge. Don't let the body rest ever. Don't ever slow down. Remain youthful. Stronger and more sinewy than anyone. Forever young. Protected.

I like long trips. I like being on a long-haul flight or riding a cross-countries train, the white noise of people's flaws, facts, and farts a cementing glue factored as a nuisance to be minimized like the drag of air on wings. These are my Neverlands, shared transports in an economy of scale. I entertain these zones where I can forego human contact. As is engineered for in these situations, I turn to blind, happy to be buffeted from the ground as much as to be on the move, prodded by blasts of roaring winds, escaping, soon escaped. Body: mid-forties. Mind: a fretting teenager, a talc and tantrum baby, depending on whom you ask about me.

As long as I toured, I had no age and the calendar pinned on my kitchen wall remained that of the year 2008. It wasn't until four years later that I bothered updating it. If I keep running, I thought, I'll catch up to my bandmates—of legal drinking age anywhere but the States, Iraq and Mongolia—and be as new and indestructible as they were back then. I crisscrossed Europe with my revolving cast of long-limbed boys, looking for relief from myself. One November, we played thirty shows in thirty days, and were convinced this was the life. What was there not to like? Heard and paid, applauded, I mattered. When I asked for unsweetened, organic, crunchy peanut butter on tour riders, I got the jar I requested, unopened. Every night. I had joined the brotherhood of the suitcase clan. A strange camaraderie indeed, like truck drivers who wave to each other as they pass on the highway, we occupied the same circuits, playing the same stages in venues across Europe but rarely on the same bills. Ships in the night, we met by chance in airport lounges or scribbled messages for each other on the graffitied walls of backstage green rooms. Member of an elite Euro jet-trash traveling sales force and I loved it. In Beijing, I took a selfie in front of a giant wall. On it were portraits of the festival bands looming ten feet high at the entrance of the festival grounds. I laughed. My mug shot was splashed in between Ludacris' sleek smile and Thirty Seconds To Mars' metallic grins. I was an absolute nobody in China. Standing below my blown-up self, I felt like a pirate breaking through a forbidden strait. Was I French, was I American to them? On stage that evening, and the following day in Shanghai, I wasn't either and yet, I was alive and I commandeered my bewildered audience.

Six eggs to go and I'm not even on that plane yet. I reach inside the handbag strapped to my shoulder to frisk the eggs and I get slightly nauseous. They're still warm. Feeling the eggs under my fingertips suffocates me. It's an odd, queasy response of the stomach to their still-warmth, a gag reflex to the tepid heat and the small-grain sandpaper grit of the shell. I cup one egg, grinding my teeth, reminded of a most peculiar thing, Vine-worthy. I've seen Cat get freaked out by a boiled piece of chicken thrown on its plate, the white breast still hot from the range, the lifelike temperature of the lifeless meat a conundrum on a plate, maybe even a threat. I can't tell if she overplays her instincts for kicks, can't tell how much she truly believes this piece of chicken is alive and, being alive, a possible threat. Games of chicken do spice up mealtimes, though. As rage played out for theatrics soon dies down on a soccer field lest the game not go on, so does the temperature of the meat eventually align with that of the air around and all is well again at feeding time. Now it's me who's confounded by the artificial warmth of inert egg matter, the potential danger of suspended life resumed ghoul-like in a processed item: cooked through, hardened, simple. Boiled from fragile to dead, from viscous slurry to travelable oneness, crucibled. Under my fingers, the eggs grow in size inside the bag and take over its folds and the recesses of its pockets from my passport, wallet, phone, hair clip, and pen, and the paper printouts of my boarding pass, bus ticket, the directions and instructions to the rental house, a book, and the dictionary. I roll an egg under my fingers. It's disgusting. It's irresistible.

Someone pinch me. I'm not a freak. I'm not nobody. Back in 2008, badly bruised from a dragged-out split, awkwardly single, as uncomfortable being labeled a divorcee as I had been a wife, I gave myself over to working and took to the road to forget. Forging ahead ragingly with a first album, then months of touring, immediately followed by a second album and more widespread touring, I was bent on redress, a formidable engine for extirpating myself from the old skin. This is how the narrative went, and then looped on itself. I wanted revenge against anyone—including my ex—who had ever attempted to hold me back from telling my story. Revenge against the injustice of being a woman, trapped, as I felt then, by a condition I didn't choose, didn't particularly like, and didn't understand. I didn't say these things, was not aware of the depth of my reservoir of anger. I toughened up, erecting a wall of mysterious and baffling behaviors that turned off practically everyone. More manly than the men, more ambitious than most of the musicians I knew in Tucson, I learned to play a woman on stage but greatly feared being one outside of show time. Womanhood meant motherhood meant death. The split with my ex had ended on a very bitter note, with my swallowing an abortion pill that I didn't spit back out. I was torn, to say the least. Could that have been the one? Could I have gone through then with that deadliest of prospects: motherhood, the ultimate trap?

By the time I recorded my third album in Tucson, I was

lost, drained, staring at myself nightly in that bathroom mirror, despairing, depleted, lonely, and suicidal. Running away from seeing myself as a failure, I traveled far and wide and made it easy for myself to disappear. The more I was applauded for my work and energy, the more I hid my true feelings. One invitation at a time, one TV interview after radio show, I grabbed onto a new lifestyle and became who my label, my publicist, my booking agent, and my bandmates needed me to be. With no child, no man left behind, I skipped across oceans to set foot on three, then four continents. No country was safe from my stage persona. In the deep country of New Zealand, I shocked a small-town audience by showing a rape scene I had filmed as part of a Warhol-inspired cowboy film we had shot in Tucson. On my Beijing festival stage, the organizers asked me to cut down on the swearing. My performance had puzzled the audience, some of whom, uncomfortable with the unwomanly rage I displayed on stage, inquired whether I was both drunk and high while performing. Neither one nor the other, I was simply banging my head on the walls, rattling the bars of my own cage.

"Flight 7301. Calling passenger Dissard. Please proceed to your gate immediately." I fast sit down to peel egg number one. Playing chicken with my egg. Who's going to break down first? Egg doesn't cry. Now who wins? Egg lets itself be tampered with, its shell be crushed to bits, the gelatinous whiteness exposed and a massive yellow engulfed. I barely chew it.

Happy birthday, whispers the gate-checker as she hands back my French passport. Stunned to be reminded of something I'd already managed to forget—the mind is a waterfall—I have nothing to say in return. No thanks, no fuck off. I tuck the passport away alongside the American one—my two allegiances in burgundy and navy blue, and take a step forward with Cat into the engorged funnel corridor to our plane. I hate birthdays.

4

I WAS UNDER THE gun to grow up. Year after year, night after wasteful night in that Tucson bathroom, I took refuge under the sink to heave tearless sobs and, post-deflating, spasmodic, disembodied and hollow, I found it harder and harder to stand back up and breathe. Things were not looking good. By 2013, desperation had become the loose, stained pajamas I wore 24/7 around the house. When, on the evening of my brush with blindness, it occurred to me I hadn't even been conscious of losing my sight, I glimpsed how much danger I was in, living in a baffling state of complete deflection between my head and my body. At last, blinded, I understood it might be terminal. Having entered the final stage in the escalation of a Cold War between me and myself—and knowing it—I got more careful. For a few days, anyway.

In my case, the more heartfelt the evening resolution

to cease and desist from self-harm, the shorter it lasted. The next day, the hurling would start again, worse even, a howling backwash against my most sincere aspirations. Now doubting my very hinges, I began to think of the ways I could end it all. Yes, what could be the easiest way to terminate myself? Gas seemed the most practical, poetic, protracted, and painless. The kitchen whale, a restored 1950s classic white stove bought off Craigslist, had a large oven with a door flipping down long as a crib and pilot lights sputtering plenty of warmth into the room on those rare but bitter cold days in the desert. I loved that stove. Unpractical, temperamental, the antithesis of the microwave ovens I never owned, the venerable double-width O'Keefe & Merritt required as much careful monitoring as a patient on pill watch, lest a gas leak set the house on fire. When I would go to bed knowing all pilots were churning blue, I'd fall asleep imagining they'd go out during the night and the seeping gas, first resting heavy on the bottom, then filling up the kitchen, then the whole house, would silently reach the bedroom and slip into bed with me. On those occasions when I left town for a few days, Cat, no canary, would of course know to steer clear of the kitchen until I had returned and rebooted the pilot jet, clearing the air by opening all the windows to the creosote-scented breeze.

* * *

Thump, thump. Copious applause from the passengers cocks up the end of our flight and stirs me from my Tucson reverie.

We've landed. It'd been a rough couple hours in the plane. Maybe it was one too many kicks of my absent-minded foot to her carrier that had set Cat off? She had panicked a few minutes into the trip and bit me through the mesh when I tried to soothe her. Was it the unrelenting plane noise, the vibrations, or gravity's pull lessened that unhinged her? As for me, I was cringing at the smell of fear dripping from a hundred armpits. Cat didn't enjoy the flight at all, but I didn't have it in me to worry about her. Restless myself, I couldn't sleep or see beyond my own discomfort. I would pick up *Arrière-fond*, the book I had brought onboard, and flip it open to a random page. But, looping from the end of one single sentence back around to its start, I only managed to drain the French words of their meaning by staring fixedly at them. Too depleted to make any sense of the experience, I soon closed the book. A minute later, I'd reopen it. Stewards were ushering carts down the aisle. Cat would moan. An angry and confused baby, I needed a pacifier but the book wasn't doing it. I thought of Tucson and felt unease. I ate two more eggs and didn't speak a word to my neighbors. Home. Hearse. Europe. Even the blasts of turbulence that shook the plane as we approached Paris failed to stir me out my numbness or dilute the hatred I was always feeling for myself and my body.

Who's that girl? A progeny-free single divorcee who's berated and battered herself plenty through her entire adult life. So much so that she needs to retreat to her parents' home for a while, to find shelter on the continent where she was born and raised until the age of sixteen. Yes, Little Girl, what now? Are you looking for a haven from the storm upcoming? Did you smell it coming? Did you see the skies turn to black? Is that why you left your home in America? Where do you belong?

Greeted by a *bonjour* as I hand my French passport to one of two cropped heads behind the thick glass of an immigration cubicle, I take the nationality test feeling like a cheat. French? Yes. Dead? No. Alive? Depends on what you mean by that. "*Bienvenue en France*." Thanks. Quiz aced, I step forward, put on the country-appropriate mask of the perpetually weary and mildly exasperated by pursing the lips and rolling the eyes. I am glad for the dapper midday sunlight, not for the spunk and warmth it brings into the hallways through the immense bay windows, but so that I can justify to myself wearing the sunglasses that hide my ugliness in public, that shield and isolate me so I can remain hub-level anonymous and chafe through the terminal, past ersatzes of French bistros and grapes of machine-gunning tots toward my train.

I've been convinced for a long time that no one can change. I'm proof of that, living proof – if living is what that circus act amounts to. Proof enough that hope is useless. I haven't been able to kick off my dangerous habit in all these years. I will never change. Only thing that matters now is keeping steady. Do not burp when the china set is balanced on top of your skull. Do not giggle under the surgeon's blade. Hide or the ripper will whiff you out. Catholic halter-girl, I'm still of course prone to feeling lots of shame and a huge amount of nondisclosure of secret practices washed away by tearful ritualized repentances. And who's going to admit defeat? Not this stubborn child, overachiever me. Yet I do feel like I've failed at a few things—making a home in Tucson, having a normal life with a family brood, being a success as an artist, being spiritual and funny, beautiful and loved, mastering French cooking and clothes-mending. I've come home for shelter, although that would take another long while before I can admit that to myself. For now, I'm busying myself with yet another new project: yoga certification.

From Terminal C, I get onto the RER B train to Paris, a forty-five-minute ride. The doors slide shut; we've been hoarded. The train's mass hugs tight to the rails, swallows them under its weight. I glide, we all glide forward. When two stations later at Parc des Expositions the compartment gets filled front to back with suited bodies tagged with credentials for the 13th Intl. Food & Nutrition trade show, I get squashed between the glass of a sliding door and two sales reps, smelling of sweat, discussing with studied casualness the merits of a new protein shake. I should really have taken a taxi, but I'm tired of making decisions, and although there is no great logic and zero practical advantage to taking a train instead of a taxi, in this instance I went with the inertia of a good resolution gone awry, that of trying to save money whenever I can. This train ride costs twelve euros, a taxi fare closer to forty. I'm lugging around an animal in a carrier, a large suitcase, a backpack. What am I? Superwoman? Good thing I don't have kids or they'd tearfully be making that point right now. This is stupid. I'm about to spend twenty-five hundred euros of my parents' money for a month of yoga practice while living rent-free and gloriously alone in a big and comfy Paris apartment they own—and used to live in—and I pay for it by suffering through a train ride because it's cheaper than taking a taxi? What kind of way of the cross is this? It's a first-world problem, that's for sure. I guess I feel guilty—mostly confused—about money. Love too. Family certainly. Womanhood. Life. If only I had known to pray for a sense of humor, maybe love, life, and the rest of the foot soldiers would have picked up their stone-filled rucksacks and hit the trails again.

Train B southbends on rails running as certifiably parallel as heaven and hell. I am surrounded by humans. Cocooned by their warmth, I tune out all thoughts, close my eyes, and take in these bodies' sheer presence in space. Gorging on the heat they radiate, breathing their scent, I hear their heartbeats resonating in my own chest. I can't escape from this train. I can't escape people. By some miracle, surprisingly grounded by the proximity of human bodies, I feel at peace for an instant, one passenger amongst many on this hell ride. Softened by the unlikely fire, I relax through another few stations. Soon enough, Cat and I will be landing at Gare du Nord, Train B's first stop in Paris. Welcome to a big city.

5

I'M THINKING ABOUT LOVE as I pedal along boulevard de Magenta to my first day of training. Well, not so much love as about entanglements of the romantic sort. I'm in Paris, world capital of padlock pledges, a place where motions of love end up fastened to the metal loins of stoic monuments and to the ventricles of bridges stretched over a river that's never just called "river" by natives but *la Seine*, seen as it is with its pompadoured chestnut trees and lurking barges.

Obviously I am not in love, or I wouldn't find heart locks tacky. But I'm tangled up all the same. Smog-trapped troubadour whizzing down Magenta on my bike, I'm cynically waxing poetic between Louxor and Lafayette over a two-block stretch of the boulevard that has, as far as I can remember, always been lined with wedding apparel shops of discount bridal gowns and groom outerwear on sale at a splashy ninety-nine euros for the stiff crow suit. My wedding dress didn't cost that much. It was borrowed from a collection of vintage dresses that my mother-in-law, a fine-art painter, had amassed over the years in her attic. I picked one—the only one I could slink my waist through and zip up without tearing—for a series of photos I thought American immigration would be needing to see to believe my marriage was for real.

I don't miss being married. A while back I marked the end of that chapter with my first two tattoos—a small bird in black ink on the inside of my left wrist, and on the right wrist, a hollowed heart, thin-lined in black ink over my artery. Each celebrated the recording of, respectively, my first and second albums, the bird likely in retrospect a symbol of my new identity, that of a singer. As for the heart, it had been my husband's band logo. I decided to make a statement and tweaked it, removing his name from the design but keeping the heart shape. After each inking session, I'd stare at my wrists countless times throughout the day, proudly showing them off to strangers in line at the grocery store. I wrote breakup songs but these two tattoos were worth a dozen of them. Was my ex shocked or hurt when I showed him the new ink of his excised logo? I don't know. At that point, we were beyond repair, but it felt good stating it in indelible ink and move on. The bird tattoo had served the same purpose. The disruptive love affair whose end it marked had not destroyed me. I would wear its ink not quite privately but proudly.

Berating from my bike lane the lovers—and tourists—who think it cute to padlock their dreams to Paris bridges, I don't feel like a hypocrite despite my wrist chains of permanent ink. More likely, I just don't really see any more what the fuss is all about. Love fades, love goes away, and that's it. There's nothing permanent about it, so, I ask, why fool yourself with iron locks. Better to know it and act preemptively to avoid getting hurt. Oh, that's ironic. Me who coos around the world for a living, delivering these songs of mine with the French lilt that threatens to turn any lyric, no matter the subject matter, into a declaration of passion. Me, the romance language peddler of love songs, I'm looking from above at romantics. No, I'm not a hypocrite, but at this stage in my music career, I might very well badly be in need of new, grown-up material.

After a twenty-minute commute, I dock the Vélib, my rented city bicycle, at the bike station across boulevard Voltaire from the Bataclan Café. With a bit of time still before class, I go in and order a *petit noir*. The place is quiet at this hour. A woman is washing the floors, and the barista looks wearily at the bright morning light teasing the room. I like this café and the feel of perpetual hangover it displays as a badge of honor. This is a late-night establishment in a noctambule part of the city, most lively at closing time when concert-going crowds overflow from the Bataclan venue next door. On the left of the café, there's a small tattoo shop, and around the corner, a narrow one-way street where, in a courtyard behind the Bataclan building, my yoga studio is located. The tattoo shop is closed at this hour and the marquee is blank today—no shows tonight. On this quiet morning of spring 2013, many months away from the horrific attack that spilled over this sidewalk from the venue, it's a beautiful day in the neighborhood. Café, bicycles, yoga, tattoos, and a music venue on one city block. This is familiar territory, no matter what the city. No wonder I'm sniffing around these parts as if, deep down, I recognized a safe harbor, a place where I belong as a tattooed and singing yogini, a social, coffee-drinking, music-loving animal. The combination of terrace tables, neon marquee and yoga studio reminds me of the Tucson downtown where all these comforting things were already mine.

Turning the corner and hurrying to the studio, I wonder if the professor will recognize me. I've taken dozens of classes with him over the years but it was long ago. Why would he remember me? A discreet, undemanding, and self-managing student, I never said much to him, and hadn't tried to stand out. I was as good as wallpaper. Opening into the courtyard, the staircase leading to the studio fascinates me, and I'll find myself lingering there longer and longer each day. No one pays attention to it, yet it's a hiding place in plain sight. Without a light bulb, it is just ten narrow steps where shoes are stored when space becomes scarce on the shelves. It becomes my own private cave during breaks. By contrast, the reception area and the practice room are bright and airy, as befits the modern yoga space, with tall windows the length of the room that flood it with sunlight until noon. It's a discreetly elegant, multifunctional, and practical space. The afternoon light is reflected back into the room by the freshly whitewashed building across the alley. The ceiling frames wide exposed wooden beams. The two rooms are simply dressed, spotted by the touch of color of an orchid and, notwithstanding a small Buddha statue, devoid of the Sanskrit engraved planks or asanas poster found in the American studios I have visited. It all classifies as *à l'ancienne* IKEA, a sort of vernacular Esperanto spoken on both sides of the Atlantic.

Shoeless, I check in by signing my name on a plain sheet of white paper placed down strategically, precisely, and discreetly on a ledge at the entrance of the practice room. I'm anxious enough that I worry about the piece of paper as I handle it. Will it keep on its ledge or fall over during class because of me? Who will pick it up? Will they point a finger in my direction? I try to shake the thought away. Happily, the check-in process is light on bureaucracy. Just a pen and a piece of paper. The work starts there for me, with having to remember to sign in daily. Attention to detail matters, and instructing the hand to affix a signature is the first gesture of the class, one that requires my full attention, one I'm afraid I'll forget. I've always liked first days of school best. At least then, something out of the ordinary is keeping me on my toes. Isn't that why I've been doing yoga so obsessively? To keep each practice feeling like the first and, by extension, each day?

★ ★ ★

First days? What was it the American teens saw when I dropped mid-term onto the ground of their high school campus? For three trimesters beginning in the fall of 1985, I was first the new kid, then the skinny French chick. School had been back in session for a couple months already and, as the one fresh face of the month, I stood out even more in the hallways. Making my way to my first class, I wasn't yet aware of the existence of cliques. The kids were just strangers to me, all of them alike, strangers doing strange things. Would I pledge to the jocks or the cheerleaders, the straight-edge crew or the rockabilly kids? That wasn't the question yet on that first morning. Should I join the gaggle of goth kids, greasers, or drama geeks? I didn't see any difference yet. As I entered the classroom that first morning, I only noticed the size of the soft drink container a very skinny girl held to her chest. She was sucking hard on a two-foot straw, slurping loudly when the plastic cup became empty. Extra Large—a new American-English term I learned that day—and extra void of anything but caffeine, such was her daily liquid breakfast. I later learned it was Diet Pepsi—mid-80s Phoenix was not Coke territory—and that it was this girl's wake-up and keep-burning kick. She was not alone in the ritual—there was a whole regiment whose members cut through all denominations, creeds, and colors: the clique of the self-starving ones.

⋆ ⋆ ⋆

I'm limbering in with my blue yoga mat. Thirty, maybe forty students have already claimed their spot around the room and laid down their mats in neat rows. The professor walks in and urges us to take our places. I choose to set up camp about four feet away from the wall, unroll my mat, a travel version weighing just a couple of pounds and well worn from use. First-row placement is a hiding tactic. Only the wall can look me in the eyes while I pretend to be the star student, the eager one. We're about to start. I haven't spoken to anyone yet, just trying to get through this morning without being noticed. I unfurl on the floor, discreetly stretching. I let out a sigh, but I'm about as relaxed as a live wire, on the edge like that piece of paper, precariously balanced on my imaginary steps to hell.

We're now told to sit up straight and close our eyes. I breathe in. It feels like a massive effort. And the first class starts with the collective exhalation of the Om sound.

6

AS INSTRUCTED, I'VE CLOSED my eyes, palms of hands pressing gently but firmly against one another with thumbs resting on my chest at the heart. Well, technically below and off-center from the heart, mine at least. I try to empty my mind by listening to my breathing and noticing how my chest—all right, my heart then—rises against my thumbs. My mind wanders, however, and I keep thinking of the back alleys of Palermo, the six eggs and that night, that night back in Tucson.

* * *

That night, as I soaked away my troubles in the bathtub, the thought of suicide had reared up once more from the water like the only sensible solution to the helplessness I felt. I was too exhausted to keep fighting, and way too distraught to keep pretending to myself all was well. I just have to stop me, I thought, now deeply convinced I would at last find peace only through death. Not named at first, depression had advanced masked for months and months, parading undetected and masquerading as inertia, numbness, and silence. Cat, leaping onto the edge of the tub—and balancing herself admirably well—unruffled by the giant pink salamander she saw in it, proceeded to dip her tongue in and lap up bathwater mixed with flakes of the dead skin I'd been furiously scrubbing away from my stinky body.

I sank lower in the tub and inserted in my thoughts the logistics of dying, relishing the comfort that familiarity with any subject brought me. I've always liked to build things and undertake new projects from scratch, and this one frontier was looking more and more worthy of my efforts. After studying the land map, I was ready to stake my claim. Night after night, I had been circling the wagons, settling on the spot where the wooden axle of my chariot lay fractured beyond repair. *'Tis all well we fall there. 'Tis as it is*. The settlers, I dreamt, would mouth those words as a mantra as they waited for their final hour, having wandered just far enough along their route for all hope of surviving another parched day on the trail to have evaporated. Resigned to my fate, I too was making a home on the field of permanent disappearance. The joke was on us, though. Without fail, under the miraculous rain cloud that dumped life in buckets, there shone beyond that last hill the promised cities of gold or the land of milk and honey.

Every night, Cat would get on the edge of that bathtub and

drink, and every night, I'd look at her, blinking super fast, trying to stop the motion of her tongue so I could finally understand how she did it. It never worked. I never got to the core of that mystery, never saw with my own eyes that what cats do is curl up the tip of their tongue to cup the liquid. Her tongue always looked straight as it went in, maybe narrowing a bit and I thought that Cat simply must be inhaling the water. It looked magical. Some weeks later, I finally looked it up online. They cup. It was all in my head, the inhaling. They cup. There were still mysteries around, Eureka moments. Maybe I shouldn't.

★ ★ ★

In the studio, Oms rise in unison from our throats. I am jolted. Where was I? I'm not Omming. I've remained silent without even realizing it, hearing but not following instructions. Where am I? I am in my left thumb, painful under the bloodied gauze wrapped around its swollen base, remembering the thrust of sharp teeth—ah, Cat, you dig deep when you bite—cutting into the finger like a blade. I am my left thumb. I replay the pain, the plane and I remember the panicked but contained look of the stewardess when I raised my bleeding hand to ask for a bandage. Embarrassed that my blood dripped onto my neighbor's lap, I still enjoyed the fear I caused him and the turbulence I created. What useless maneuver, what desperate ploy, Cat, biting me through the mesh of her softcase carrier. Confined in a plane that emits stridently high frequencies we humans can't perceive, Cat rebelled at last. Why, oh why did I ever think it a good idea to bring Cat from Tucson? Couldn't I have left her behind? How selfish of me. I'm guilty.

One and the same, home and Tucson had become traps and nothing more. I realized at last that I was only going to be getting worse if I didn't change something, so well had I managed to isolate myself from friends and family in that last-chance desert pit stop. I'm not sure to this day what cinched it but on one of these nights, maybe looking into Cat's eyes, I decided I had to do it. I had to make a run for the border. I couldn't just leave my beat-up self behind, shed by suicide. That wasn't what I wanted, not yet. I had to do something drastic, a shock therapy or it wouldn't register in my fuzzy head. Leave, run away. I had to get out of Tucson, my home of twenty years. What nailed it? A flicker of awareness, my head out of the sand just long enough to be able to assess the massiveness of my own bullshit? A spark, yes, but for what flame? Someone requiring my help, a loved one? Not that either. Cat never finding another like me? Right.

What was it then? Why did it matter to me that I changed? That I stayed alive, and beyond alive, that I be repaired?

Om. With the sound of its final letter bouncing around dozens of nasal cavities, the Om tapers off, and our professor speaks. "Please get down on all fours. Spread your fingers." I open my eyes then. Start of class and I'm out of step already, a failure. I feel shame, embarrassed as if, during a concert, I'd missed the beat and failed to reenter my own song at the moment I'm expected to open my mouth and sing.

* * *

That's when it started. That night, with Cat silenced by a sardine, I recovered from my bit of a bout with bathroom blindness and sent an apologetic email to the Phoenix venue where I was scheduled to play the following evening. Sorry, sick. Reschedule?

I knew I had to get better. Standing on a stage mattered enormously to me. I had no choice but to change because I hadn't gone into this racket to cancel shows. It had taken me some years to conquer the fear of standing at the microphone and facing an audience. By the time I get to Phoenix—goes the song—I might be old and gray, but do I have a choice? I had to get rid of the heavy baggage first. A Phoenix bird? Not so much that night. A pile of ashes still, I had reneged on a promise to a venue, my handful of fans there, and above all, to myself. I wasn't used to failure in public. Not this A-student, first-born, and her parents' pride. Grounded, not rising, as it happens, not getting to Phoenix—at last maybe a parent to myself? My pride was hurt and my shiny toy put away.

Help? I tried to get logical about it but where would I start? Yoga? Yes. More yoga might help. How could more of something good be a bad thing? Spread your fingers evenly. Breathe in. Round your back. Yes, like a Cat. Good. Landing like a cat on all fours from the great airless, my yoga mat softening the impact then anchoring me firmly in my own body. Go deep into yoga, go deep into something, anything at last. Sounds like a plan. Body knows that. Mind just needs to shut up. Now breathe out deeply. Drop your belly round and low. Like a cow. Now back to cat. Yoga can't hurt you. It never has. Maybe, yes, just maybe, yoga is the only thing you do with yourself, to yourself, that hasn't been hurting but helping. The only positive, self-loving thing.

When I started practicing yoga in 2004, all was perfect in my life—or so I liked to pretend. Back then, I never let it bother me that I would get stressed out at work, not this girl and not with these rarified jobs I have. Girl's got the perfect life with a French husband more than willing to induct her into the echoey halls of marital bliss. Perfect everything. All well, all fine. Smooth sailing. Certainly not aware of being depressed, I'd been well provided for and, at age thirty-five, had not an ounce of extra fat hiding anywhere within a pristine body. There were those who said I looked younger than my age. I wasn't even particularly touched by that compliment. I felt like I was indeed younger and my body just did what it was supposed to do. I'd always been flexible somehow, without much effort, as if that is genetically coded in this medium frame. Regular jogger, swimmer, I'd been spared much. I'd not screamed at the edge of my bed in childbirth; not been in a car accident, broken bones, or ever met a gun. I'd not been hospitalized except for an overnight stay once—standard safety measure in the well-funded French system of health care. I mean, a whole twenty-four hours for a simple abortion? That's overkill, I thought then, always acting the tough girl. Those visits to the doctor were bleeps on the radar. Blink twice and you missed them. Married, with my own house, a vintage convertible gold Cadillac in the glorious and dusky years of one-dollar-a-gallon gas. And yet the cracks were there already and I never gave them the time of day. I was fine. Come to think of it, as I was about to become a singer, the only thing I thought I needed help with—and asked advice on—was breathing.

7

THE DAY BEFORE YESTERDAY, before six eggs en route and my first Oms in Paris, I woke up to Cat pacing on the bed. We were in the apartment I was subletting in Palermo from an American friend conveniently gone abroad for some months. This is where I would return after a month of yoga training.

I liked Palermo. A hybrid of oasis and port, it was, I thought, just the type of feverish and sexy mess I'd been used to and loved from my Old Pueblo outpost in Arizona. I also liked the apartment, a minimalistically-decorated one bedroom, with beat-up furniture thrifted from the sidewalk vendors who peddled daily in the piazza below. Nesting on the fourth floor of a fifteenth-century palazzo, the apartment was close to the Vucciria market and to the port. The monumental marble staircase made me want to linger in its cool obscurity. I didn't know my neighbors, and no one in town knew my address yet.

Relocating to far-flung Palermo, a grandiose wreck of a city, as sunny and hot as I could get for cheap on the southernmost outskirts of the European continent, I would be able to lick my wounds in peace and reinvent myself as a happy girl.

By evening though, I was spitting blood. Had I made the right choice in leaving the familiar surroundings of America for this old world refuge?

Seagulls, church bells on the quarter-hour, yes. From the street below my window, an angry shout, cars idling, stuck behind a bassy garbage truck. Cradling Cat, I got up smiling from the bed, but by the time I got dressed, the sweet song of honks, bleeps, and gulls had faded. Mindlessly pinching the skin around my belly as I put on my sweatpants, looking for layers of fat that might have amassed overnight on my jaws, I stopped noticing where I was and started to remember what had happened the night before, and the night before the night before. In the brief moment it took me to walk to the kitchen from my bedroom, I had switched to panic mode.

In the kitchen, I popped out two Levothyrox pills, twice my prescribed daily dose of the thyroid-kicker molecule. I've always been a very timid drug user. Lucky me. I've never tried heroin—too afraid to lose complete control, certain I could not survive it long—and I don't enjoy smoking weed. Only once did I ever try coke, and I danced mostly alone all night on the Villa Medici terrace in Rome, sad at dawn that no one from the party, strangers still despite midnight well-wishes, would join me for a picnic in the famed gardens. Mushrooms, speed, peyote, poppers, and acid, I flushed them out of my system along with my teenage curiosity and never made the effort to get high again from either them or newer toys like Molly or

Dove. Alcohol, the legal high, felt less complicated to justify, more socially integrated, normal, even healthy, to the French kid I was. Also, I liked that there was much less blood on the whiskey trade routes than there was on the back roads winding from the Mexican border into Arizona. Even legal prescription pills, antidepressants and uppers, I proudly refused. While living in Tucson, I grew adamant about not using mule-traded drugs myself, the way vegans would cringe when I'd provocatively happen to mention that I ate and enjoyed foie gras. My friends all suspected I had zero vices, and I liked to agree with them. Uneasy around me as a result, either because of an intuition I was not being honest or because it called into question their own vices, the friends I had were many from many circles, but distant.

This Levothyrox business was ludicrous. I had no idea what I was doing. The only solution I had to feeling down, tired, jetlagged, confused, depressed, and helplessly alone was to double my daily thyroid pill dosage? What a girl. If only that trick worked as an appetite suppressant.

I smiled for about three seconds that morning, then blanked out the rest of the day, bracing for the inevitable. At dusk, I stood on the terrace watching paper lanterns rise in a blotted sky beyond the line of the furthest tiled roofs. Cat was on the ledge, trying to wrap her head around a new reality. Palermo? How did it sink in for her?

Be right here, right now. I made an effort to feel the temperature. It was warmish, a late spring evening in Sicily with just enough movement in the air to want to wear something gauzy on the shoulders after the sun is done for the day. I looked beyond the rooftops in the direction of the sea and saw a sky lantern rising high above the water. It disappeared, and I imagined it had disintegrated, or crashed at the foot of the teenage boy who had launched it from the beach. The boy had cursed the seagulls as they attacked the paper weakling. Seagulls like to peck at the meek. I've seen them dumpster-dive in the narrow alley below my window. Seagulls, rats, pigeons, stray cats, and me, we'll peck at anything, and there is plenty of good waste in those bins, enough for all of us scavengers.

I used to forage through dumpsters in Tucson before I knew there was a name for it— freeganism. It was an adventure in back alleys, a noir mystery. I never knew what I would find rummaging through the trash containers of round-the-clock supermarkets. Day-old loaves of sliced white bread, post-expiration date tubs of Philly cream cheese, donuts in pink and purple hues. Rarely did I find things I would normally buy and eat. I had been living in America for ten years by the time I looked up her skirt going through those dumpsters, but deep down I was still a foreigner. Bacon for breakfast, Cheetos for lunch, and popcorn at the movies?

The beachfront was out there, the dark sea out of reach. Launching sky lanterns? Would I have wanted to try it? Would I dare? The question distracted me for a bit from the strong metallic taste in my mouth. Pure mechanics of air and fire, the paper bags lifted, I imagine, by the heat of the candle burning inside, lifted for a moment then given the kiss of death inevitably by the flame. And on and on, out there on the horizon, the lanterns rise and hover, and zigzag down. Rise and hover and, at the whims of coastal winds, x-and-y their descent, semi-chaotically, inexorably, gloriously down to earth. Maybe that's how Icarus stumbled after his Discovery-like ascent. The fall is never swift. It plays out in slow motion and from many angles. I watch them from a distance of several city blocks, distracting myself with questions I can't answer. How many eyes on those lanterns? Are seagulls afraid of them? Should I go inside? Is the sky falling on my head?

Up on that terrace, I was getting to feel dizzy—really dizzy. A fresh breeze, though, felt good for an instant on my forehead and I rose up in thoughts to where I might be in peace at last, a place where I wouldn't have to fight anymore. Where my body did what my mind knew was best to do. Where my mind didn't go where my body knew best not to go. Where one talked and the other listened, one moved with the other, not against. One loved and the other basked in that love. Without effort, without will nor pain, body and mind as one, as promised by yoga and given by the kiss of air on my cheeks. Less is more, I say and I pray. Less is more, more harmony to deaf ears. Obliteration or happiness, I couldn't tell which was which but just this winter, I'd have taken whichever came first to me and got me out of Bumfuck Egypt, aka Tucson, aka myself.

Twenty years and I had grown insular in this town in the middle of the Arizona desert that I had learned to love like a mismatched mate. Now I needed to tear myself away. Traveling for long periods on tour, divorced, and growing older in a place where maturity is a disease of the skin and a sin against your friends, it was the right time to go, and without delay. Help was in Europe, where I came from as an untroubled teenager. Maybe the solution was in going back to where I came from, to retrace my steps and find that uncomplicated kid again. I had changed when I got to America, embracing blood-sucking aspects of life, as an immigrant bent on survival would. Go more native than the natives and wear their colors. Yes, it was time, high time to grow up. For the shock therapy I needed, for this bout of reverse engineering, I had to first get the hell out of Dodge, as the outlaws would say.

The taste of blood in my mouth wasn't going away. I felt cold and tight and felt the breeze closing in. I went from watching the sky lanterns pull a shuttle to eyeing seagulls jackass a couple of gutter cats three floors down in the alley behind the palazzo, cats and birds scouring the same bursting trash bins. I didn't look at them for long. Peering down made me feel even worse. I never used to feel vertigo but those days were over. I would start out feeling lightheaded, and feel the walls closing in. And if I was near a ledge or looking down from a window, I would be afraid and fascinated. Cat could do it and land on her feet. I might too. I had lost track of how many lives I still had to play with. Probably one, hopefully two.

I was thirsty for orange juice now. Or, maybe even more than OJ, thirsty for plain, simple, zero sum, painless water. OJ was too dangerous, too sweet, too acidic. I went back inside and walked to the bathroom. In front of the mirror, without looking into the mirror, I brushed my teeth gently with the soft tip of my right index finger. I passed it over my gums, using a drop of xylitol toothpaste. I had read in an online pro-bulimia forum—"eating disorders a lifestyle choice, not a disease,"—that xylitol is good for your teeth and you're not supposed to use a toothbrush after an episode or whatever that thing I do is called—the ritual that's not; my stupid friend; my religion. I didn't have a name for it then. Looking into the mirror, I checked the corners of my mouth for signs of cracked skin. Good. There weren't any. My cheeks were swollen, though. So was the area below my jaw, from the glands up to the middle of my neck. My eyes were swollen too, lids puffed up as well as the bags under my lower lashes, blue and sagging skin. Eyelids were specked with a hundred tiny red dots from the blood vessels that had popped while I was bent over the toilet bowl several times throughout the day.

★ ★ ★

I don't believe the sky lanterns look any different on their way down than I did then. Blistered, cracked, deformed, and blackened. Maybe it was time to stop climbing too. Maybe I had been outspending my time fighting through the trash bins. Maybe I should try walking away from the ledge. I should stop moving altogether, maybe. Learn some names, remember them. Make friends. Keep them. Maybe I didn't have a clue on how to fly graciously through the air without tearing up in flames. Icarus had landed. Through the apartment, there was a sudden chill from the wind. Maybe I was not conscious of the ascent, or the descent, and from start to finish I had been sleepwalking. I was mixing my metaphors. I'd been, I was still then a goner.

Maybe I should just say it as it is. I'm junkie material. An addict. My junk is food. I eat, dream, sling food. Food is my gunk, my needle, my sash. I puke. I puke with the single-mindedness of a marathon runner. Anorexic from the age of sixteen, purging bulimic from the minute I started living alone at age twenty-one. I've been racing that loop for twenty-five years soon going on thirty. The loop is only getting shorter around my neck each year, but by now I'm what you'd call Olympic material. A spindle queen. Deep throat athlete of the sphincter shrug shot.

★ ★ ★

The lanterns have landed. I'm crashed. From this town too, I had to get out.

8

WHEN AT THE AIRPORT, always, I hobble around the terminal, window-grazing past newsstands, a gourmet deli, the trough-feeding chains of entertainment. Get something. You're not complete. Get these sunglasses. Yours are not worthy. Eat, drink! Gift-wrap a fragrance for someone, anyone. Show them you're generous and loving when you land, that you are lovable.

Lovable? Purchases of luxury items and the nonessential gifts are frivolous. I learned that as a child, when my parents, who both came from little money, raised my brother and me while writing down every expense in a small accounting book. When, five years later, my second brother was born, the situation had changed. There was money, a lot more of it, but it came without a manual. To that generation of men and women born in France during World War II, in a small provincial town in Auvergne, for my father, and a farming village near Pau, for my mother, expressing love and speaking of one's own needs—conceits I was subjected to in school and by my friends once I moved to the States—was not something one learned growing up. So with new means to purchase things, love became things given and granted, more and more as the years went by and my parents' lot in life improved with a move to America.

I walk past a repetition of gates; screens and chairs, suitcases in black clusters or in white isolation, a tearful couple clinging. I turn left, pretend to myself I'm getting lost. If only I could get lost. Now a tired placemat *sans* dull cutlery, I have neither ties nor lies, husband nor asides. I've lost a few good eggs in my procreative years, placeholders on the walk of shame through the stations of my womb. Tossed along the way in this and that trashcan, good progenial eggs now fading Post-Its on the whiteboard of regret. But however I choose to frame it, that life coated in myriad diversionary refractions, it all leads to this departure lounge and I'm staking out my territory, the two or three nooks of the airport lounge, a bubble that rings out dizzyingly with words I don't understand from people I pass who speak languages I never will. Baby-Babel. I turn right, another left. I become familiar with the territory. I have to do it fast, make my home fast, any home, and pretend I'm comfortable there.

Once upon, when we still lived in Tucson, I followed Cat outdoors as she headed for her daily stroll around our downtown neighborhood. I trailed her through the yard and the ocotillo fence, across the neighbor's dirt lot, the one that resembles a piece of desert with its lone saguaro cactus and tumbleweeds. Cat veered off course to steer clear of the pesky barker to the left, slipped momentarily behind a prickly pear at the sound of a passing car, then rounded her steps, returning home with her heartbeat sped up by those itsy scares planted along her path. Every day that route was the same, subject to minor adjustments from flippancies of traffic and weather. In this mild version of the great outdoors, Cat rarely encountered another feline—word spreads like pollen in the feline kingdom, invisible boundaries precisely drawn in the dust around this one regal animal. This route was her route and on this bit of soil, she etched herself repeatedly. Daily, she climbed the wooden utility pole across the alley and from her mast, having silenced the woodpecker that drills there, slid back down, always birdless. *Tac, tac, tac*. Cat never got to the woodpecker on the pole but never gave up trying. *Tac, tac*, out and about, and up and down. It wasn't about the bird. Sleep, eat, and then sleep some more. Cat didn't need more than sunlight and a bit of water, dreams of a bird, and the occasional slaughter of life. Harmless thrills.

At the airport terminal bookstore, a young child is standing mesmerized in front of the shelves, head tilted, squinting to decipher the words written on thin spines. Who's watching over her? She looks to be by herself but she is not lost. She reminds me of myself, enthralled as a kid by books and so eager for the stories inside them that I would have my mother drive me every weekend to the public library, where she would leave me alone for a whole afternoon. There, I would walk the aisles until, picking a book by its cover, I'd enter a new, extraordinary world I could inhabit for a few hours. As in a fairytale, there was nothing I could not transform, no one I couldn't bend to my will. I was Harry before Potter even existed, a dream machine so powerful I knew no mundane life and didn't see walls to my cage. Cocooned by stories, I felt enlarged and ready for anything the world might throw my way. Or so I thought.

Someone was watching over me though. The day I asked to check out Nietzsche's *Thus Spake Zarathustra*, I was told by the librarian, in an opinion seconded by my mother, that the book was not for me, that I was too young. I didn't contradict either of these women nor wondered if they'd read the book themselves. There was a limit to my magic powers, and a rulebook to what nice girls could read. So I dreamed myself a Cinderella, a fasting saint, or Snow White, and I tried to understand how a little princess could be ruffled sleepless by a tiny pea under a stack of mattresses. I yearned for Prince Charming, and I kept yearning. Years later, as a teenager, I still only wanted a Prince. I couldn't imagine any other type of relationship. There was shame in public displays of affection, as I learned when I saw my parents pull apart one picnic afternoon when they noticed I was watching their modest embrace. I was not much older than three or four then and it is one of my first memories. A few years later, the Prince Charming of my dreams, a perfect mate because he wasn't made of flesh and blood, morphed into a Jesus type, the near-naked man on a cross slightly more virile maybe but still very safe thanks to the nails that kept him securely stuck to the wood. At the onset of my teenage years, I climbed to the flat roof of our house and lodged a small cross-cum-Christ in a corner, secretly visiting the recess and liking the elevated fervor I got from staring at the manly figure. Some weeks later, growing bored with the lack of response to my hankerings, I brought the cross back down and looked into trading my pink-cheeked celluloid princes and lost wax kings for real flesh Pinocchios.

My final winter in Tucson, thanks to Cat's diligent gifting,

I had started a collection of carcasses: half-eaten sparrows, mangled and gutted, bottomless lizards with wide tongues, doves half-blinded, eye sucked out and hanging, still as corpses but for the remaining pupil pulsing. The lizards' bellies in death would have turned an electric shade of blue, the color of fear. They do that, I hear. After I took photos of them on the very spot in the house where they were deposited by Cat, the corpses ended up in my freezer where they dried-out and shrunk over the following months. Kitchen, bedroom, bathroom, these were habitual settings for my gloomy displays. The red shag carpet of the living room became an exquisitely contrasting backdrop for green-gray reptiles, meticulous scales, and a loose hair: a fascinating study in textures as I moved in closer with the lens, chin on the surface of a floor that said to me, "You live here, and these are your scabs." One afternoon I even found feathers—feathers only, as the body had been disposed of—on the wooden floor of my music room, neatly arranged in a circle about one foot in diameter. The lines of the oak wooden planks were intersecting this layout in the most pleasing way. I wiggled a good place for my camera and snapped holding my breath, not wanting to disturb the surprising arrangement. *Kitchenbluelizardbellyup#26*, I named the file and later tweaked the shot in Photoshop to turn it into the cover artwork for my new album, *The Cat. Not Me*. Like the twelve songs I had recorded for Cat, the photos were a study in contradiction. "Tender yet abrasive," a critic wrote about the songs. The photos were like that too: a mangled baby bird, big eyes wide open. "Melodramatic, but vulnerable. Comical and heartbreaking."

* * *

Ask me now in which fairytale I'd like to partake and I'd choose to be the Red Hooded babe or Hansel, impressed by both their clever stratagems—white pebbles to show the way home and force-feeding stones to a wolf. Stuck on a stroll routine, fairy-queen-me would have meandered through a dark wood or two, and labyrinthed into dead ends, run along long glass corridors and found myself at last after making wolf's stomach burst with rocks. Dropping off-white bits of eggshell on the ground like so many place markers, spaced just right, the first one a step away from the second, and the second a glance away from the third, I would be sure always to find my way home and, just like that, be safe again between my enclosed walls. This wasn't to be now. You can't really stake your claim in an airport maze with bits of eggshell. You are being watched after all. Greedily monitored and held in closed circuits, but not in a proscenium sort of way. They watch bodies for a living, the security forces. They watch how you move and twitch, looking to nail you as one of the bad guys. You are bad. Why else would they watch? Pigeonholed and scrutinized, you are scanned, stripped, and made to fit the part that justifies the surveillance. Which belt is explosive-strapped? What age a suicide-bomber? Me and my eggshells. I can't drop them by the perfume rack in Duty-Free or inside the full body scanners as I lift up my arms, or under the conveyor belt at security. Anything suspicious on your body or an odd smirk at the right moment, that one word too many, the organic tucked alongside the wired in your carry-on and you're bound to be exposed to identity scrutiny, the mighty scrutity. How could I not want invisibility?

Dropping hints—and eggshells—is a game with consequences. You will be found out. Littering and loitering between terminal gates is airport roulette. What will Security think? And the cleaning crew? Oh, the paranoia is real. What if… maybe you can go ahead and scatter your shells along the way. It's a matter of proportion. You just have to be discreet about it. Have I learned these survival tactics from thirty years of life in America? Discreet living? Being flamboyantly obvious about whatever it is you're doing? One and the same in my fairy world. I'm forty-five. A woman. Places, and analyses, it's written as "45yo female," which means I'm at war with—when I'm not home in—invisibility. So I hopscotch along unattended and pace myself from one egg to the next on my way to the French capital city. Be your own maverick self. I learned that in the American West.

9

HERE WE GO, SECOND day of yoga training. I am unfurling my mat as our professor walks in, limber and lean in blue sweatpants and plain white shirt, looking fifty to his sixty-one years. Leave your mats where they are, he asks and motions us all to sit in a circle. The noise level in the room rises, then drops as dozens of bodies shuffle around to settle back down in a fairly round wall-to-wall circle. Not bad for a bunch of strangers suddenly faced with the request to act as a unified group. We had it easy on the first day, going through a yoga class that felt just strenuous enough that—focused on doing it well and bombarded with Sanskrit names of poses—we could keep in relative isolation one from another on our respective mats. Mine is a blue travel mat, thinner than average, foldable as well as rollable. It is constructed differently too, with layers of tree rubber, eco-friendly to boot. I've had it with me without fail since my first concert tour in 2008. Worn out in spots from years of almost-daily practice, the mat is home to me, the underlying white thread exposed where I planted my heels and the palms of my hands. Lined as uniquely as a fingerprint, wrinkled from hours of friction and buckets of sweat, I show off my mat. Yes, people do take notice of its storied state, but more often than not, they'll simply ask where I bought it, tired as they are themselves of carrying their thick mats around town and country. Thin, blue, worn-out, suitcase-ready. That's my style.

After his grand entrance and dramatic takeover of our attention, our professor—*le prof* as we call him— joins the circle and we fall silent, ready to drink in his careful words. Teaching is a performance. What a wonderful skill it is to be able to command attention from the very first step you take into a classroom. I realized that when I worked as a substitute teacher, the first of many part-time jobs I held in Tucson—like selling roses and waitressing—that required a level of showmanship and self-confidence that I didn't have when I started peddling burgers, romance, and lesson plans. Today, from my place in the circle, I count fifty, maybe sixty of us. I don't know anyone by name yet. There are so many of us. My eyes darting from body to body, I look for tell-all signs of who these people are. Are there any members of my tribe, anyone with tattoos or quirky hairstyles, tattered sweatpants? Any Americans, or even just the odd, relaxed leg-crossing self-styler? As I look to make sense of this circle and understand whether I fit in, I'm starting to feel like a bit of a chameleon again, looking for ways to merge in, blend, and disappear. Granted, this is not my Tucson yoga studio. The professor isn't tattooed nor anyone around buffed like Olympians. I would feel safer being like everybody, but I don't know what "everybody" means here yet. I'm back in France. I'm confused. Just a few hours ago, I was in Palermo, and a few weeks ago, I was in Tucson. As I do when I feel overwhelmed and threatened, I begin to wander in thoughts and notice the rapid-fire burps of a jack hammer coming up through the open windows. I listen and see patterns, and know the particular feel of the echo rolling through the chamber of the courtyard. Mid-sized, lower end, crackling sounds of the city.

★ ★ ★

On my first day as a twelfth grader in America, fresh off the boat so to speak, I also found myself in a class circle. I remember it well for it was an uneasy moment, with Kevin and John who insisted they should be addressed as Vito and JJ, Linda as Yona, and Deborah as Debsy, all strange names I would have to get used to if I hoped to make friends. In our homeroom—a new concept too—after we sat through the garbled loudspeaker announcements and stood for a pledge whose purpose rattled the French in me, we were asked by our teacher to move our desks and form a circle. We then proceeded to introduce ourselves to the class. But first—and this is where it got tricky for me—we had to repeat the names of everybody who had spoken before us. My turn came in halfway through the circle and I had to remember more than a dozen names. First, Anna, got that one. Then… JJ and Shaun, Sean, and Brenda or Brandon…. Hearing foreign names, some for the first time, I couldn't quite figure them out, couldn't see them spelled out in my mind, which is how I would have been able to nail them to memory. I grew more and more embarrassed at not being able to perform the exercise as requested. What did it say about me? I felt like a failure but truly, I hadn't been hanging out with these people for three years, five years, all my life and yes, these were new faces, new names, new monikers, a new language. Oh, to burrow deep under my desk. I don't like group circles. Might be why I never made it to an AA meeting for disordered eaters. Not my cup of bitter tea, this circle thing, nor is waiting in angst while others speak.

* * *

Three, six, nine, twelve... fifty-one, fifty-four and.... Yes, I was close to guessing. Fifty-five yoginis. That's a hefty class. Fifty-five times two-and-a-half grand? That's *beaucoup, beaucoup* euros. Not a bad setup. But really? Are we all here to train and become yoga teachers? I didn't realize Paris was such a boomtown for yoga. I first heard about this studio eight years ago when it was suggested by one of my Tucson teachers whose own teacher had practiced there. I heeded the recommendation. The studio's founder, our professor, has been practicing since 1969, and teaching since 1981 when he introduced the dynamic style of Vinyasa yoga to France. From the time of my first visit, whenever I was in Paris, I made sure to take one of his classes. They always made me feel good and appeased like no other classes I had taken. Transmission, in yoga as in language, is by deeds and rote, from one person to another, and lineage matters.

Teachers the world over are liable at some point to assess—and advertise—their degrees of separation to the great, original Indian masters: BKS Iyengar and Pattabhi Jois, Sivananda Saraswati in Rishikesh. I had not ever been and would never be in their presence. Joking with my teachers back in Tucson how I was having an intercontinental fling, repeatedly being unfaithful to their spacious, luminous downtown studio with a middle-aged, decrepit, drafty, minuscule and sunless Paris studio, I was in truth also loving the two degrees of separation from the great teachers, now all deceased, that the proximity to their student, my *prof*, afforded me.

Joining us in the circle, the professor introduces himself but makes no mention of his impressive pedigree. No guru talk or enlightened wisecracks either. The short speech feels rather straightforward compared to how such an introduction might have sounded back in the States. Even the way he is sitting on his mat is humble, as far from fakir-like showmanship as I can think of. Any of us in the room can do what he's doing with his legs, a loose Lotus, as he explains how the course will unfold over the next month. Actually, I don't recall what the professor tells us because, sitting about three quarters of the way around the circle and with a good fifteen minutes before my turn to speak, I'm already fretting about what to reveal of myself and with what phraseology. I quickly take notice of the gender composition of the group but pay little attention to what students say of themselves. There are unsurprisingly only a half-dozen guys in the room. Ten women to each man. Whether in the States or Europe, that's a reliable ratio.

Fifty-five students and I want to feel special? I've only ever been in a yoga class that large in cities like Los Angeles or New

York, in studio rooms converted from spacious lofts or hangars. Of course, I know Paris is a big worldly city too, and hip to all things that animate us back in the States. Still, that's a lot of people for a training. Somehow, maybe because my first class a few years back had been held in the original, small studio room, I never imagined this training would be so… inclusive? Eight years later and the professor doesn't look changed from when I first met him, clean-cut and steadfast with the same small-framed, rectangular glasses—the very same pair, I was ready to guess. Bursting into an easy smile, he doesn't offer big laughs or angry words. I used to marvel at the photos of his much younger self in intricate poses. Framed and hung around the studio, the stark photos spoke of a time not so remote when yoga wasn't trending on YouTube, a time before world competitions and copyrighted asanas sequences, before red wine classes and, yes, Goat Yoga.

I still don't know what I'm going to say to the group. Should I tell them why I started yoga? Or why I'm here? Certainly not. Hello, my name is Marianne and I'm a recovering—but no, I'm not recovering or recovered from anything. I hear the first step in recovery is to come clean to yourself, and I'm not quite there yet. I scan the bodies in the room, looking for tattoos and anything out of the ordinary like a peg leg, but everyone seems intact, plain and healthy, lean in that French sort of way where women are gracile and wispy, and men just buff enough in comparison. A blonde lady in her late thirties across the room from me is fidgeting. She crosses and uncrosses her legs, straightens her back, sighs. Her turn comes and, blushing, she just says her name then signals with her hand to the slender brunette sitting next in line, who tells us she works in an office all day and she hates how stressed she is at work. Her husband wants her to quit. There's a muscular man with a southern accent, maybe from Marseille. He tells us he's a fitness instructor in a private gym chain and has been asked to add yoga to his menu of classes. Another guy, in an Adidas sweater, explains that he was hurt in a skiing accident and has yoga to thank for being able to hit the slopes again. Next is someone who might be the youngest of us all. She looks transparent, her sleek brown hair hiding bony shoulders. I don't know how she's going to withstand the training. She seems so frail, anorexic probably. She waves her turn, refusing to speak. I'm intrigued by her silence, but I don't know if I like her. I might not like anyone here. I'm not like any of them. Stress, broken bones, ambition, and shattered dreams? I would never admit to any of that in public.

My turn? My turn. Oh no. I close my eyes. Shaking inside, I keep silent for a few seconds that feel like minutes. Now I've got to come up with something. *Think fast. Don't cringe, don't crinkle your face. Smile inside*. I slowly breathe in, and out, in and out again but it's not helping much to slow my heartbeat. *They're looking at you. Waiting for you*. Then, out of the blue, an idea, this off-road strategy. Eyes still closed, I take a deep breath and, slowly and deliberately, let out the Om word, rolling out and stretching best I can each of its three sounds—the A, the U, the M. The wavering wavelengths sputter from my mouth, my throat, my lungs, my belly, my core. I hear the sound echo through the room, spill into the courtyard, fade out, and all is silent again. I open my eyes, see the large room, me in it, and faint smiles. Hello. My name is Marianne and I'm… I pause. This isn't an AA meeting. I'm here for Om. This, this sound

Om, to me, it is the hardest thing to say, to do. To do well. Sure, we all know how to do it. We've done it so many times. I do it mechanically at the start and the end of each class. But it is the hardest thing to get right, I mean, harder than any of the physical poses. Just opening your mouth and letting this out, clean and full. A breath. Life.

Om.

I did it. Wallpaper-me shimmied away from the wall for a moment. I said what I had to say and I tried to make it something. My Om, sweet Om.

10

THAT NIGHT.

I clear my throat and bend over. Beige juices first through the mouth, then a torrent of mush gushes outward. Gastric droplets explode out, splatter against my thighs and the rim of the toilet bowl. My insides are massaged by the shift of cubic volumes of food—the sensation is not unpleasurable—or is it my abs that heed the push? Expulsion suspended, the muscles of the torso relax. The abdomen aligns down to its resting position, diaphragm lowered, and the ribs stack back inward, allowing the lungs once again to expand and contract, as they must. Breathing resumes.

But I must keep at it, keep pushing out as much stuff as I can—as much as is in there—and I do it again, and again, do it as many times as I can without ramming both my index and middle fingers past the tongue and down the esophagus.

These are the preambles, the part of the negotiation that goes down easy. On good days, I managed to ingest a helpful ratio of liquids to solids, something like half and half, and can throw up the entire content of my orgy without once shoving my hands down my throat. It does take a bit of muscle control though, a certain tightening of the core and coordination of diaphragmatic breathing with the expulsion. But if the retching goes smoothly, I'll look up the bowl and into the mirror without the unmistakable tell-all red dots on both my eyelids and upper cheeks, the spots where blood vessels have burst from inside pressure and muscle tightening. Also, the fingerless mode of puking preserves the nails from corrosion by stomach acid, and it also saves me from looking like a chipmunk the next morning, my underjaw swollen as if I'd spent the night squirreling a bunch of nuts in my jowl.

About once every couple of years, I get a full-on shiner—might be over the left eye or the right—that's beyond my control. The first time it happened, I made up a story about running into the corner of a kitchen cabinet while putting away dishes but in truth, the deep raccoon rim smacked of wife battery or if I'd fist-fought bigger than myself—and lost. Most times, though, the pin-dotted eyelids just swell up and I see white specks float in my field of vision, the consequence, optical this time, of powerful pressure applied in bursts from within to the optic nerves. Yellowish gunk streaks across my pupils and bunches up in the corner of the eyes. If I'm lucky, things stop there before temporary blindness. My heart, so far, has held up. The corners of my mouth are eaten away, cracked like a bad cold sore. The skin of the index and middle fingers of my right hand—the digits I shove down my throat—is dry, and their fingernails brittle. The circles under my eyes darken and eyelids puff out. Raccoon eyes are my trademark feature by now and, no, these dark circles are not from a rock 'n' roll lifestyle of sleepless nights, booze, and hard toys.

It's a noisy business, this puking. To hide it from neighbors on the floors above and below, as well as anyone who might be using the creaky staircase at that instant, I've started up my iTunes. The entry door to the apartment, directly adjacent to that of the toilet, is not well insulated, and the sounds of footsteps and voices reach in as much as out. Some tracks work better than others at white-noising my toilet operations. Today, I've put on the mp3 of Sedaris reading one of his short stories, "Turbulence." As the author tells of his time in an airplane sitting next to a woman who actively dislikes him, I wonder if, instead of Sedaris, I shouldn't turn on the shower. The jittery sound of water coming down from a showerhead effectively cancels out mid-range voices and some types of bass-range coughs. I'd need the shower on for ten, twenty minutes, the length of an episode from full to empty. That's a lot of good, clean water to waste, and today I choose to not turn on the shower. I like how the Sedaris story started and want to hear it through. I like the sound of his voice and the mundaneness of the story. Nothing happens in that plane, but he makes his time there sound so eventful. Today, inexplicably, I feel guilty about wasting water. Maybe it's something I read earlier about water being the new gold. Thoughts at this juncture of an episode—what I call my "commercial break", when I might get up for refills—are jumbled like a radio dial gone rogue, scampering off and on signal. News of the world and song lyrics mix unprocessed in a brain soaked in chemicals. Carbon credit is water credit is a staircase to heaven. I saved the world today and the doomsday clock ticks this diabolical jig, perfected over many years—my dopamine Tarantella. No, I don't feel guilty wasting food. Like a rat starved too long of corn and company, I take what is there, tomorrow be damned.

That's not true. I do, I do feel guilty. I feel guilty about everything.

And ashamed. Very, very ashamed.

* * *

Remember the wafer-thin mint?

When I first saw Monty Python's *Meaning of Life*, I laughed a lot, but especially hard at the final scene. In a fancy French restaurant, a very big man in dinner jacket, Mr. Creosote, has eaten, eaten, and eaten. Despite being "absolutely stuffed," he says, he eats one wafer-thin mint and explodes. The content of his stupendous stomach is splattered all over the restaurant. A poor little heart still beating inside the big, hollowed, exposed chest, Mr. Creosote is ceremoniously presented with the check for his gargantuan meal. When I binge, there always comes a time for my wafer-thin mint. It is the last little morsel I can swallow and I never know which it will be. Could be salty or sweet, a cracker or a pea. At that point, before potentially catastrophic gastric rupture, I barrel out of the kitchen to bend over the toilet bowl and, in that moment, remember something one of my teachers once told me in class. "You're very flexible," he'd said. "Resist going there, where it's easy. Work to pull away from the ground." So I unbend a bit from a near perfect fold-over and use the muscle power in my legs and core to gain better access and control of my stomach muscles, the very same muscles that I use during yoga breathing exercises and digestion-enhancing twists. Not unlike Mr. Creosote, I can't resist eating the wafer-thin mint. When the check comes due, however, I look the other way.

★ ★ ★

On those days when the package doesn't come out smoothly, I have to resort to further tricks. I drink a glass of warm water and quietly wait a couple minutes for the water to mix with food stuck in the esophagus. I might repeat that step one or two times if the flow doesn't improve. If I have pants on, I drop them to my ankles and, grabbing a towel, place it near the toilet bowl. I lift up the seat, if it isn't up yet. Maybe I've had time already to tie back my hair away from my face. If not, I do so then. I bend my knees further and place my face just above the bowl so my torso is almost horizontal. I wait a few seconds, breathing as deeply as I can, then start contracting my stomach muscles to get a feel of where things are stuck. If the situation is dire, I use a sort of Heimlich maneuver, pushing my fist into the esophagus, while pushing with my butt against a wall or the ledge of the sink.

When stuff comes out, in a river or as rocks, I notice its quality. Textures, colors, and shapes give me clues on which foods have made it back out. It's an odd study, like an archaeological trash-diving experiment on the tastes of people from the past. From these clues and markers, I can tell how far I've reached in the process, which I want to complete to the utmost emptying of my belly. For some physiological reason I don't understand, the first morsels that are swallowed tumble out last, as if digestive churnings were some sort of washing machine spin cycle.

Is it pleasurable, though? Maybe, on a physical level, only as much as the pleasure I'd get from taking a large dump, when a wave of relief ripples through the body. Are they one and the same—excreting feces and vomiting—when it comes to massaging the internal organs? Contraction and relaxation of muscles in the forced expulsion of matter sends a spasm of soothing shivers throughout the body, a gratifying exercise in tension and release. The signal is loud and clear at that instant; body comes first. Some days, nausea shortcuts and takes over the process. On those occasions, at great pain to walk, skin stretched taut over the belly as if pregnant with a herd of balloons, I don't even need to use my fingers and the overriding, automatic reflex of repulsion takes care of business as naturally and powerfully as, for a birth, the pelvic floor of a woman. Retching feels as if it's the most vital release, the only essential thing in my life, a necessity, an obligation, and an achievement. The successful coordination of these bodily actions is a thing of beauty, muscles directed by thought to perform a choreography of rehearsed steps and undertake the inhumane task of self-harming.

★ ★ ★

I take a break again, stand up and, grabbing the towel that's been set there for that purpose, wipe the edges of the bowl and remove all splashes from the wall. My glasses have been off my nose, and I look for them, sometimes for a while, too myopic to spot them at once and too frazzled to remember where I might have put them down. Again, I flush. I can't smell anything yet but I already know I have to get rid of the stench I know to be there immediately or it will linger in the apartment overnight and repulse me with shame when I wake, able again to smell. I wash hands and face with soap, scrub my arms too if they've been reached by vomit. I swirl warm water in the mouth to dislodge remaining bits of food. Cold water will hurt my teeth and hot water will hurt my throat. I drink room-temperature water, a glass at most, to dilute whatever bile is left in my system and minimize the damage it would cause there, where bile isn't supposed to be.

But before I can rest, before sleep and vague but heartfelt promises of "never again," I have to go back at it one last time, for one more round. I won't stop, I can't stop until I've heard that one last particular retching sound, the hollow one that tells me there is nothing left down there to bring up, that I'm all cleaned up and pure again. I need to hear that sound. It's the only certainty I can grab onto to feel whole again. Like the floating marshmallows you'd wait for at the sewer plate looking down into the pipes—a real estate agent's trick to verify connection of house to network—I'm back at it, hoping to see the very first meal of the day float by. Most days, breakfast was healthy, wholesome, and eaten in peace some twelve hours ago and I want to taste it again. Peace. From white—the color of flour from the sweet and buttery boulangerie treats that dominated the first round of vomiting—to this brownish-green specked with black dots—the cumin seeds I had sprinkled on the rice and vegetable dish I had for breakfast, yes, there it is at last, the signal that I'm done. Thank you, little black seeds. Now I can wash hands and face one last time, forget what just happened and re-enter an atmosphere of chamomile tea and late-night TV series.

★ ★ ★

This after-the-fact chilling is a step I take as seriously as a breath-hold diver would the surface intervals that ward off decompression sickness. I veg out on the sofa, shaken still from the in-out workout, and think as little as possible about what I've just done. Forget. Forget it happened and, comfortably numb, forget to despair it has happened again. To equate bulimia to the highly skilled sport of freediving is coarsely flattering for this couch potato. More bluntly, I'd say I am just like an alcoholic, but I've spent so many years feeling so deeply ashamed and worthless that I actually look up to alcoholics as highly functioning social beings, enviable adults several steps above my own shut-in condition. Billie Holiday, Lorenz Hart, Townes Van Zandt? They all made a mark on music while I haven't. So what if they died of alcoholism? Mine was hardly a glamorous group to belong to. We couldn't claim the sexiest fuck-ups. No Jim Morrison in our midst, no Kurt Cobain—although we have Amy Winehouse. For every *Barfly*, *Withnail and I*, or *The Lost Weekend* I've watched, I've steered clear of Hollywood films with bulimic characters. Were there any during all these years? Except for Mr. Creosote, that most spectacularly endearing of sickos, I know of no companions of fortune, not in la-la lands, not in my own lane. Fairer to say, even if said companions in distress were thrown onto my lap, I still wouldn't recognize them. When the cult indie film by Todd Haynes, *Superstar: The Karen Carpenter Story*, came out in 1987, I watched it with much interest, but not because I felt like Karen's struggles had anything to do with my own. I looked at the film with the appreciative eye of the filmmaker I was and, in complete denial, not as the sick person I had already been for several years.

Tonight, my hopes are slight and my dreams modest. Please, let me fall asleep fast, and sleep without waking. And in the morning, let me be hungry and not look too beat and blue for class.

11

NINE O'CLOCK THE NEXT morning. I am back on autopilot. Having sliced half of a red pepper, some kale, and a broccoli stalk, I slide the pieces into the pressure cooker and scoop in exactly a hundred grams of quinoa. I crank the range to its highest heat setting, close the lid. In twenty-one minutes, the content will be ready to transfer to a Tupperware container. By nine-thirty, I will have headed out the door for day three of yoga training, and I'm already looking forward to the healthy quinoa/veg dish I will have for lunch.

I have to have healthy—and safe and boring—food for lunch. Anything other than my talismanic quinoa stew, meaning sugar spikes and remorseful pleasure, will set me down, I fear, on the path to yet another evening hugging the porcelain bowl.

As the pressure cooker whizzes, I pour myself a third cup of yerba mate, spike it with green stevia powder and unsweetened soymilk. The hot brew turns beige, sweet, and acrid the way I like it, although most would find it repulsive. Pure, green stevia tastes like grass. Yerba mate is also an acquired taste, swampy and bitter. With soy thrown in the mix, my morning perk-up drink is an odd one, but I find it comforting and, more important, unlike coffee, my battered stomach can handle it.

How did I get here? Yerba mate, quinoa, stevia, these are a far, far cry from the kitchen staples I grew up with in 1970s rural France. No one that I recall was in the least worried about where their food came from and whether it was healthy. But food was crap in America. My last high school lunch in France was green beans, mashed potatoes, and a small ground beef patty. A week later, my first high school lunch in Arizona was—my choice—either pepperoni pizza or a cheeseburger, both with fries and ketchup, and strawberry milk or chocolate milk. Truly, this was the land of free choice. The food was colorful, fun, and very sweet. It was also very unhealthy. In a few weeks, I fattened up and slowed down. Although it took me a few years after I moved out of my parents' home, I had to learn by myself and for myself what healthy eating was. Right around the time I left Arizona to attend college in Los Angeles, the guiltless-eats late-80s precursor to Whole Foods, Trader Joe's, was already on the map, but it wasn't until I moved out of my kitchen-less dorm room and without the meal plan that came with full college tuition that I had to learn to use an oven. Trader Joe's was convenient. One of its very first stores was located two blocks from my first apartment in downtown Culver City. I graduated from diet sodas to the novelty fresh carrot juice that was sold there, and from ketchup back to Grey Poupon, one of many French basics Trader Joe's would be ingraining on the

American psyche over the following decade.

Spirulina shake after green grass shots, I got wiser about the relationship between food and health, to the point where I thought of myself as a fully educated eater and a halfway-decent nurse, tinkering with food to heal colds, allergies, and yeast infections, and maybe even the onslaught of nastier diseases. In truth, I was becoming someone who rightly estimated the calorie count of every bite I ate just as I'd learned to guess the number of jellybeans in a jar, or the final cost, to a dime, of my shopping cart. These things will get you far in Los Angeles.

Only when I moved to Tucson at the age of twenty-five did I truly fall in love with Mexican food. All the ingredients were there, plentiful and cheap, and I welcomed huevos rancheros into my daily routine. Imported Gruyère cheese was too expensive to melt over quesadillas. I learned to love *queso blanco*. Over two decades I grew to think of corn tortillas as my everyday sustenance, yet I held on to a hardback thrift store copy of *Mastering the Art of French Cooking*, Julia Child's classic treatise on my native cuisine. At times, I leafed nostalgically through it while cooking. Child's detailed descriptions of soups and sauces, desserts and mains, using words that spoke of smells and tastes I faintly recalled from childhood, brought back memories of holiday meals at my grandmother's table. I never used the recipes to cook for myself or others, but I liked the language and appreciated that so much care could be bestowed upon food. I held on to the book like a talisman, a link to a past I hadn't really known but that was oddly more real than my own childhood experiences in France. Eventually, I had to get rid of the book. It was one of the last things I sold during the last of three yard sales I held in the weeks before leaving Tucson for Palermo. A few people had asked to buy it, but I couldn't bring myself to give them a reasonable price. Finally, the kid who convinced me to sell it to him had been most persuasive. He explained that, although he was for now just a line cook in a Mexican restaurant, he would become a great chef someday. I gave him the book for free. Maybe that way I'd be skipping town having made a positive difference in somebody's life. At that point, I was so desperate to leave Tucson that I was unable to see how many friends I still had there. Violently tearing myself away, I couldn't feel sadness at leaving. Tucson had to be the enemy, not myself. How inoffensive it was then for me to think that some kid in a Tucson kitchen had been altered by a tattered and cherished book of mine. Everyone else—old friends, bandmates, neighbors, ex-flings, and favorite ghosts—I had already renounced. I couldn't feel, I wouldn't feel—sadness, regrets, love, joy, or simple happiness. If I had done, unable to deal with the pain, I might have gone blind, die, or, more embarrassingly, become another Terri Schiavo corpse.

★ ★ ★

There is no Julia Child bible in my Paris kitchen now. Since waking up, I've made two batches of quinoa. I ate the first for breakfast, flavored with a favorite—and peculiar—mix of cayenne and stevia. It made me feel good. Now I look forward to lunch for the same desirable outcome: a feeling of fullness, satisfaction, a lack of desire for anything extra, a roadblock on the path to bingeing. Evenings, thanks to a comforting dinner of quinoa once again, the third batch of the day, I might manage to jump straight into the harness of sleep without getting ravenous and lightheaded. Let the days be uneventful and my blood sugar even. The humdrum of flatliner foods like rice, corn, or millet, and of course, my favorite, quinoa—all grains that are easy to digest—is what I aspire to when I wake up and when I go to bed. Let my food, let my life be unprocessed, unadulterated, and boring.

Brownie points for reckless, blind ambition. Did I have any idea what I would be getting into when I signed on for twenty-eight uninterrupted days of a training more physically challenging than anything I have ever done? Did I really think my body, wrecked by daily bulimic fits, could handle that many push-ups?

When I get to the studio at ten that morning, I'm already hungry. The work begins hard, and we sweat and roll through the two-hour practice with no break until lunch, spending a good part of the morning class on perfecting our handstands. One stiff right leg shoots up and the heel hits the wall with a thump. That's me there, practicing my handstand at the punching wall. A voice to my left. "Ooh, easy there. You don't want to…"—second thump. Left heel now crushes the wall—"to punch a hole. They just got the walls patched up last month. That's what he said, right? Take it easy when you go up." And another voice: "Okay, now push your hands into the floor. Yes, all fingers, knuckles down. Grab that floor like a juicy piece of something… something juicy. Index fingers pa-ra-llel." Damn, why can't these two geese just shut the fuck up while I'm hanging in there, head down, bile box upended. I'm so tired of the noise. All right, just breathe. Forget about these two girls hovering around. Just come down. Back to Downward Dog again. Safe place. Home. "Hey, your turns now," I tell them, "I'm done," and I go from D-Dog to kneeling on the ground. It's all yours. Keep cool. They're just being helpful, just here to work and you are too. Joy poppers in training, we're all in here to do our best and learn to do happy. Oh, my head is spinning. Crouched, butt over heels, I drop my forehead to the floor, stretch the arms straight on my good old mat and sink low to the ground, low as belly allows between my thighs, and I sigh deeply. Time-out in Child's pose. Swallow me, earth. I'm exhausted. I'm hungry and running on empty. I want to lay down somewhere out of sight, out of reach, and sleep for days. So much for learning. I can't think of anything else but food. So much for a sound body.

When I get home late afternoon after class, Cat hasn't been out all day. Cat lives in an apartment now and sadly, unfairly, doesn't get to roam, and I feel obliged to entertain her. We play mouse with a stuffed toy for a minute, but soon I am drifting to my computer. Yes, Cat and mouse was fun, I admit, but I need a stronger thrill. I'm opening my email, hoping for some bit of heart-jumping news, anything to remind me I'm wanted somewhere, and that I exist for someone, anywhere, as a singer. Page hits, email requests for an interview, Facebook likes, new Instagram followers, listening stats. Oh… an offer to perform. Ouch. My heartbeat goes up. I don't know if I'm ready for that. I don't know if I can handle being on a stage anytime soon. I'm in the middle of replying to that email when Cat jumps on the table and walks across the computer keyboard. Oh, who needs attention again? Shooing her away, I finish typing a response to the offer—a concert in a beautiful venue in Paris in just a few weeks and with a budget to fly my dream bandmate from Seattle for the night. Here we go again. I can't refuse. I can't say no, I never do. Nah, nah, I say to Cat. You were trying to stop it, weren't you? You're tired of stepping on gold glitter when you tiptoe around the rooms, and my jolly confetti don't entertain you much anymore. Deal with it, Cat. I've confirmed the date, and there's nothing you can do about it. I want it. Hysterical with anticipation, I jump up and do a little happy dance around the computer. Cat leaps down from the table, steps away to the balcony to quiz that fat pigeon forever holding court on the meanest branch of the florid pine tree that thrones in the courtyard. Cat knows. I shouldn't have accepted.

I want that date, yes, but do I need it? This is rickety. Bandmate is embarked on a massive world tour in giant arenas. We won't have much, if any, time to rehearse. The audience—guests at a film company's twentieth anniversary party—won't care a bit what we'll be doing on a stage contrived for the occasion in a corner of a 1930s movie palace that's ill-suited for live performance. I shouldn't have said yes, but I don't know how to say no: no to the attention, no to concerts, no to food, no to myself, no to being wanted and being told I'm beautiful. Oh, chill. It's going to be alright. Yes, you'll get all of that if you go through with the show. Why not take a chance? I'm excited. What else would I be doing with myself? Singing is my one magical power. From the day I started giving it my all—November 3rd, 2004—it's been a happy, scary, adrenaline-soaked joyride. I want it bad.

12

AND WHERE WAS MY soul—or whatever it's called—in all that? When did I think to check on it except when prompted by a teacher's invocation for universal peace at the start of a yoga class? Days in, days out, shaken up by my disordered living, I was neither here nor there. Neither in my body nor particularly conscious of my thoughts. Tracing and retracing the routing of our tours over maps of Europe and the Americas—finding relief in the relentless crafting of a more impervious public self, I worried little about my oneness with the cosmos.

Not that I hadn't tried to slow down. In typically half-assed self-help fashion, I had sought out a spiritual warm-up as a way to prep into receiving the wisdom of the Paris intensive. I had heard about Vipassana meditation retreats from Tucson folks whose soundness of mind I trusted. One of them, as much a devotee of our Congress Street downtown yoga studio as I was, had spoken alluringly about his experience at the silent retreats. Intrigued, I looked up the Vipassana schedule. Conveniently, there was a ten-day session set to end just a few days before my move to Europe. It wasn't held anywhere near Tucson but I signed up, glad to cap my years in America with such a closing statement—and an overnight stay in Seattle where I hoped to see my bandmate du jour. Prosaically, without daring to say it or even truly just think it, I was hoping the meditation retreat would keep me in check for ten days, a holiday from myself in a safe environment. With nowhere to run, fixed meals and schedules, and shared, privacy-less bathrooms, the center seemed like the perfect detox joint—discount-rate, gluten-free if I wanted it, vaguely uplifting and densely spiritual. I would arrive in Europe light in soul and rested in body, ready to begin living again.

Most of my belongings sold, and suitcases already packed for the big overseas move, I left Cat behind in Tucson, alone with the run of the house. I flew to Seattle with sweet and bitter herb stevia now my second-best lifeline to the familiar.

* * *

A large rural compound of modern sleeping units arranged around a gymnasium-size meditation hall, the retreat center sat on the outskirts of Onalaska, a small town nestled in a beautiful secluded valley halfway between Portland and Seattle. Carpooling with a couple of veteran sitters who picked me up at Seattle International, clogged from yet another episode of my favorite serial run-in with food, I grew more apprehensive as we rode I-5, Mount Rainier looming to our left, into the Cascadian midlands. Casting off one by one the add-ons we'd amassed in the megalopolis—salty dogs, green mermaids, sweaty Doritos, styrofoam miso, and five bars of mobile reception, we got off the Main Street highway corridor after an hour and let a Scottish-accented Sat Nav lead us through the recesses of Doug-Firlandia. Apprehensive? Ten whole days safe from myself. I should have been relieved.

★ ★ ★

I had heard scant but ultimately intriguing tales about his experience at the retreat from the yogi I knew in Tucson, who offhandedly admitted he had re-enlisted several years in a row. We spoke a few times after class outside the downtown studio, and he was initially reluctant or unable to explain what the sittings had been like. Maybe I didn't know what to ask. Was I wanting to know if he'd been changed, or cured of any ills? The vagueness of his response made the mysteries of the retreat grow in allure. I remember teasing him that it sounded a bit like running a marathon. Smiling, he replied that it was probably more painful. Sticky happy from the athletic yoga practice we'd just been through, I asked him how anyone would be able to remain still and silent for eleven hours a day, ten days in a row. To me, not moving seemed far, far more unbearable than not talking, silence a reprieve from making sense of myself and others that I always gladly welcomed. To "sit" in Vipassana meditation, I later read, was to be promised "the release of suffering through the practice of dispassion, a tranquility that fostered moment-to-moment mindfulness of the inconsistency of events." The sitting part sounded horrid. From what I understood of his account, this yogi had returned to our fold of the frying pan a more serene and less bitter man. But to me, he looked only more dampened, or was it cautious, the quiet of his character underlined by the practice, almost as if he had been chastised or was shell-shocked. I wasn't getting it.

* * *

In the reception room of the Onalaska center, waiting in line with my co-riders, I flipped open my phone one last time to check if a text message or an email had come through. There were none. I paused, self-conscious that I was still glued to my phone, and with a deep breath, turned the thing off. When my turn came, I placed the phone ceremoniously down on the table, where an eager, name-tagged twenty-something girl picked it up. "Anything else, iPod, iPad, books maybe?" she squinted. Nothing else, I offered.

* * *

As cautious as my yogi classmate about analyzing her own experience at the retreat, a Tucson photographer I met during one of her downtown gallery openings had suggested that I simply had to go through it myself. It was the only way to understand, she promised, adding that it would do wonders for my creativity as it had done for hers. She pointed excitedly to her photographs—a stark series of trees in winter—explaining they were actually mandalas. Standing in front of the frames, seeing only oddly patterned leafless branches, I wondered if maybe I wasn't yet spiritually enlightened enough to feel anything.

To neither yogi nor photographer could I disclose what I faintly hoped to get out of my system at the retreat. The application form I filled online was brief and to the point. It made it clear that Vipassana wasn't a substitute for proper mental health care or a cure for addiction and other self-inflicted delinquencies. I was asked to list any and all drugs I used (none), how much I drank (so very little, mostly), and what medicines I took (a white pill). I wasn't sure how it would affect me, but if meditation—and yoga—had made a difference in both these people's daily habits, in their creativity even, it didn't show in any spectacular ways. Was this what wisdom looked like? Was this life unencumbered of illusions? One of the things the yogi, the photographer, and I had in common besides yoga was that we had been able to drop out from our lives for ten to twelve days. With paychecks that could wait to be earned, no childcare to arrange, and, for them, understanding mates, we were able to go work hard at doing nothing.

I wanted a finishing school for the soul. I would give Vipassana a try. It might be good shock therapy. And it didn't cost anything to participate. What was I to lose?

★ ★ ★

Okay, thank you." The girl scribbled a couple of words on a loose piece of paper, tore a couple of tickets with matching numbers and handed me one, affixing the other to my bagged property. "You'll get your phone back after breakfast on the eleventh day." Our tools and toys were being stripped away. We weren't encouraged to keep up with our yoga practice while at the center. There were no spare rooms available for it. Besides, other than taking short walks at preset times and within a strictly cordoned path, any extracurricular activity was deemed detrimental to our learning. We were here to work hard at meditating. Still, in a bit of an individualistic surge, and anticipating I would enjoy landing in Paris as flexible and fit as I could for the training, I had sneaked in my travel mat. I figured I could always hide it under the bed. I was also told not to bring outside food with me and to satisfy myself with the healthy vegetarian cooking we'd be offered, but I still arrived with my travel-safe red French press and a bag of the swampy green stevia powder. The first couple of days I went through meals comforted by their use but soon came to regret not having gone cold turkey on any and all familiar items. By the end of the retreat, mat, coffee press, and stevia felt like booby traps on my path to cloud nine, obligations that I fulfilled more through sheer habit of inertia than deeply-felt need.

It was 5:00pm on D-Day One. I walked to the dining room. Dinner was being served right on time. I didn't have high expectations for it, but I was curious about the food. And what a meal. A bowl of sliced-up, diced-down fruits—banana, apple, and orange generously sprinkled with seeds and spices. Enough sesame, flax, chia, and sunflower mixed with the sweet juices to heap one lovely spoonful with a glomerate not quite amounting to but as close to solid food as I'd get that night. I was happily fooled. The meal was a feast, I did declare, and took my sweet time sucking on a piece of banana while I stared blankly into the white wall I sat facing. Behind me, the sound of plates against utensils, clanks of chairs being moved around, rattle of throats cleared. I picked bits of fruit with my fork, chewing very, very consciously.

A peaceful slab of the Pacific Northwest indeed. Within the boundaries of the Vipassana center, looking over a clearing in the redwoods that afternoon, I caught sight of deer. On a path further to the right, beyond invisible lines drawn to separate the sexes, I saw the men walking. I pondered the strict gender and species segregation at the center and found it habitual.

No phone, no computer, no books. I couldn't listen to music—no prefabricated sounds allowed—but I had kept a pen, also not permitted. I got into the habit of rolling out my mat every day between lunch and afternoon meditation, stretching in the small space between my single bed, the simple nightstand and the thin drywall separating me from my ghostly roommate. Deprived of notebooks or even a single scrap of paper, I used a white toilet roll to jot what I was convinced were deep and necessary lyrics. What if the best songs I'd ever whipped up came to me here, in this space of introspection? Toilet paper would do just fine to soak up my musings about berries and men's bodies.

Private tiny rebellions of this sort were not helping things, though. After a couple of days, these habitual concerns of mine—yoga, writing song lyrics—lost their urgency as it became obvious that time ran painfully, unbearably, poignantly slower if I distracted myself with usual obsessions. Grasping at the old, I floated through the present without focus, and, exhausted, wasted away. Meditation was hard work. To split my focus was draining. I felt unanchored. Thoughts jumped from what I should be doing to what I wanted to be doing, from what I did to what might have been. Was I no good at self-discipline? You bet. I wasn't even good at being disciplined. Blueberries and their stain, dark woods where they grow, first kiss, a story maybe, a song that will say so much in so few words? Yes, I kept writing on toilet paper, but the lyrics were unmasked a month later as counterfeit gold, crap. I stretched and twisted on my mat, keeping my attention on the breath in a movement meditation. Why did I want to torture myself? I couldn't bend over the toilet bowl, not with a roommate on the same schedule as I was, not with controlled intake of these bland foods. But my mind still ran laps. That much was becoming clearer.

Every day, as soon as the 9:00pm bell had rung, releasing us from the last mandatory group meditation, I trailed back to my room, brushed my teeth, wearily undressed and slid into bed, slumbering off to an uninterrupted, dreamless night. No puking tonight.

★ ★ ★

The gung-ho gong stirred me up at 4:00am sharp. Here we go again. I hastily dressed and made my way through the darkness to the meditation hall. Hooded figures came out from behind me, surrounded me, all of us wrapped in long, warm shawls. I was one of them, just one of them. An hour later, dawn broke in the hall and its rows of sitters. At 6:30am, a gong rang. Time for breakfast: tea and bread. Then, after a half-hour of personal time with laundry, shower, a short walk maybe, another gong signaled the need to make our way back to the hall for mandatory morning group sitting until lunch at 11:30am.

It was loud in the silent meditation hall. Creaking with the percolations of human bodies, leaky human faucets, the space resonated with misfires and filled with exhaust fumes as we trolled the high roads to the spa of the soul. Silence was a dear, deceased relative. Outdoors, the wood was awaking with birds getting down to business and not so far out there, somewhere in the middle of the morning, the dark crack of a firearm, maybe —hopefully just a hunter's rifle. I heard birdsongs and shots as if they originated inside the hall. I couldn't help thinking there might be a madman out there, nearby, with a deadly assault weapon, a calibrated tube of fire, the endgame of reason and civil allegiance, someone who thought us weird and cultish. That would explain the loud bang. It was America, after all.

Gunman alert? We were weighed down by veils of obedience, in precarious equilibrium on our wooden stools, low chairs and on our pillows. Our skulls were reaching out to the blue skies, our mental focus on the slightest movements of our nothingnesses or the pangs of hunger and boredom. Oblivious? Each and every one of us, I tell you, was right then, prompted by the sound of a firearm, gleefully running the same movie in their head as I was in mine. We were in danger. The gray thought tumbled down our spines, triggered the eternal conundrum. Fight or flight? For a split second, a nothing moment, yes, I knew it, we all saw the same madman with a machine gun, and how he entered with cocked urgency our sacred hall and proceeded to blast every single one of us, sitting duchesses in training, with cryogenic bullets. How we knew him!

What a movie, and how anxious the mind. I didn't know which of my fellow sitters were running that apocalyptic scenario in their head. In my case, it took up the rest of the morning. As I sat motionless, propped by my three pillows and wrapped in a couple of blankets, I was savior of the world. Beware, gunman. Supple and strong as I felt from practicing yoga warring stances, I was the superhero who had saved the day. I ducked and slid on the floor at the most dangerous moment when the machine gun was trigger-ready, and I sneaked up next to the madman, and bang, boom, whizz, crack, karate-kicked him into submission, pinned him to the ground, my foot hard upon his throat, crushing. Humble heroine of the day, I refused to gloat and when the media crew descended upon the compound, remained hidden in the woods. My name nonetheless got splashed all over the country and I became an instant celebrity, personifying all that is humblest, most generous, and altruistic in human nature. Then, some months later, the music video of the event would be shot by Hiro Murai to a transcendental soundtrack.

Still, I was in much pain sitting on the floor. During lunch break, I requested to use a chair for the rest of the retreat. My right knee was killing me. My left hip shot venom through my spine. I had to stand this, I knew, but… I would not, could not stand this any longer. What on earth was I supposed to do and what, for heaven's sake, was I supposed to feel? Regulations had it that I had to ask our teacher in person for an alternate sitting arrangement, making the simple request a very formal one. So I visited her at the appointed time in the empty meditation hall.

When my turn came, she waved me forward to the raised stage and invited me to sit down in front of her. She asked me why I wished for a chair. But as soon as she asked and before I could reply, enlightened, I knew I'd already changed my mind. A chair was not the solution, I told her. I described the pain in my legs. I told her that I had tried to not run away from it, that I even accepted it. Feeling proud that I had stood still through the pain, I told her I had obeyed instructions, hadn't I? And my pain, however unbearable, I dug it. All was good. She asked why I did that. She asked if I clung to the pain, and why. At her words, I realized that this was exactly what I was doing, had been doing all along. Clinging to the pain.

I bowed down to thank her for her time and left the hall. No pain? What was the point of being here then? What was the point of anything if not to be in pain? Making my way toward the woods, I strode carefully, looking after the bounce in my step. The other students were napping, some lingering over lunch. I was the only student outdoors at this hour. The deer were out again. I moved closer to the pack, and closer again as they remained nonplussed by my presence. I stood still, only a few feet away from an endearingly frail young'un. The vapor of its breathing materialized in the cold air. I was getting wet feet standing in the mud. But then, so was this shimmering Bambi. Pain? We stared at each other and I winked.

13

I AM WAVERING IN a handstand. This is the very pose, Adho Mukha Vrksasana, the upturned-down vertical balance, that has been eluding me most since I started yoga. I stubbornly keep at it. Every morning during the two-hour master class, I get another shot at cracking the code. I go lay my mat against a wall, set myself in Downward Dog, lift the right leg, and kick it up to the wall. The second leg follows, and I hang down, pulling my heels up. Day after day, I can stick out a little further away from the wall, but I'm not quite able to balance unassisted.

"Keep your legs together," admonishes *le prof.*

Yes, yes, I know.

"Belly button inward."

Forgot that one. Belly in? Remind me, please? How does that work again?

"In. Tuck it in all the way to your spine. Come on."

That doesn't sound too complicated—suck it in. But belly? That's my hot button issue and in this position right now, I don't seem to be able to connect the wires in my brain to the nerves in my core and pull a successful tuck. So I flounder again—ah, so much for the body/mind connection—yet hold the pose 'til it starts hurting and, hands gripped like claws, my hard-working head swells in pride at feeling sore in the wrists, shoulders, and neck.

But that smell? Ah, ah. There it is again. It rises from my right hand to my nose and, when I pick up on it, throws me off balance. No matter how long I scrubbed, no matter how much I scraped, the bitter stench of bile has lingered overnight on my index and middle fingers. Oh, I hope no one but me is picking up on the smell. So nasty. I'm sure they know, even all the way to the back of the room, what that means. Something primal is twitching inside their reptilian nostrils at the same time as they take good note, I'm certain, of how perfectly I can hold my Tree poses. Shh, quiet. I'm tippy-toeing on the ceiling. I look perfect. Envy me. I am buff. I am limitless!

"I have a leg that's shorter," I say to the professor in a rare admission of vulnerability. He considers it for a brief moment.

"By how much?"

I stick up my hand, separating thumb and index by, oh, about this much, "Inch, inch and a half?"

The professor thinks about it but shrugs it off. "Ah, that's nothing. We all do. We all have a leg that's shorter."

Ouch. That's the second shrug in as many weeks from revered masters, the first in our Vipassana meditation hall and now in this yoga studio. Do I really cling to pain? Do I find comfort in being different?

I learned a long time ago to shift the blame for pretty much everything that was wrong with me to my hips, or my legs depending on the day. Yes, by birth, my right leg is shorter and my knees angle inward. As far as I remember, they've always been knocking, which means I've grown two rugby calves, ghastly balloons, to compensate for these crooked legs. My ankles don't meet unless I deliberately force them to and, when I do, the arches of my feet flatten, which makes my big toes stick out. Poor hips, poor girl. She'll never find a husband.

I don't know when I first took notice—I think it was noticed for me, a kid unaware of having any mechanical quirks. I must have been around eight or nine when my parents brought me to meet a pediatrician who was to look into this *genu valgum* of mine. A year before, my mother's father had died of metastasized bone cancer, and the anxiety she must have felt then likely spread through to me. What if I was afflicted too, by genetic transmission? My case, however, was soon dropped, and the operation to help correct the misalignment of my knees was cancelled. The inward deformity remained but I had learned something new. I had learned that something was wrong with me. This body of mine was a cause of clinical concern before it was one of celebration. I didn't learn to love it. My father liked young kids—they were harmless and loved unconditionally—but dreaded and possibly feared teenagers—they were incomprehensible trouble, heartless aliens. My mother only feared babies, but I suspected she also feared womanhood—or was it sexuality altogether? Whenever I showed her a pair of high heel shoes I had bought, she would wince and mutter, "Really? Do you need those?" How could anyone not love high heels?

Oh, the racket. Racket in and racket outside my head.

Voices that spur me to self-hate, self-harm, and selfhood; I am permeable to your paranoia-inducing incantations. I grew up with an incommunicado father who expected to be obeyed quickly and with no questions asked. His growing silence and my mother's compensating chatter caracoled in my head all throughout my childhood. Breathe. Breathe now. Forget how shitty you feel. A good girl doesn't put up protective walls against her parents. Or does she? You're more normal than you think. Forget that your nasal cavity is dried up, your palate raw from scratches made by crisp bread crusts and the ridges of tortilla chips. Forget about the purple bruise the size of a silver coin on the tip of your tongue, all that remains this morning of the blood bubble you had to burst with tweezers last night when it grew as big as a hazelnut filled with dark blood hardening after you bit your tongue. Speech will be blurred for a day. Tongues heal fast. Don't speak. Breathe. You're not that far off from a cure.

★ ★ ★

I progress slowly in class despite my professed eagerness to learn. Never missing a class and always on time, up to date on the assigned readings, I am a dutiful student, not afraid to volunteer to demonstrate a pose and always willing to lend a hand to my fellow students. They must find me insufferable.

Mornings at the studio, when it takes long minutes before the patter of the class ceases and the student body settles down, the indiscipline of the class annoys me as it would certainly have irritated my father. I don't like scattered. Solid, silent, and stoic is what I need right now to maintain the fragile mental and physical equilibrium I'm finding in the bicycle-yoga-sleep routine. From my front row, I give the chatter bugs my back-of-the-head evil eye and preach the silent treatment. *Le prof* is on his mat a few feet away and sighs too. I do what he does, always one to side with the powerful, as if this was still elementary school or my parents' home.

* * *

I'm upside down, inverted on my mat, negotiating a temporary truce with gravity. This is my first successful, unassisted handstand, at long last. I'm blocking distracting sounds—keep the eyes focused on the space between your hands, or your inner eye staring halfway between your eyebrows—and the apprehension of my helpers—they're afraid, not you, they're excited and bored, not you. I hear the professor approach. My focus wavers. He exhales a loud "ah" and shushes my effusive sidekicks. *No*, I pray. *Go away*. He takes his turn cuing me, instructing me to tuck the belly and tilt the pelvis, but I freeze on the spot, ruffled by his attention. I don't want help. I want to do it on my own terms, at my own pace, and away from stares. I come back down, deflated. Attention like his makes me very uncomfortable and I desert the battlefield. I sense he's disappointed, vexed even, that I have not accepted his help, persevered. Party-pooper me, blue baller, I refuse to share my solo triumph. Why do I keep seeing these men, authority figures all in my skewed assessment, as father figures and, as such, to be protected from? Like a chameleon on overdrive, I scream: look at me / don't look at me, I'm invisible / I'm the Pantone queen.

I don't trust myself yet, but I trust work. I've always trusted work, the more the better. Come evening, I read from the twenty-deep list of assigned treatises on yoga. There wouldn't have been as many books assigned if I'd been training in the States. I pick up the anatomy manual. Despite its colorful diagrams, this isn't what I'd pull out for bubble bath time. The fairytales of mystics, medicine men, and warriors narrated by travelogist Sudhir Kakar are more my thing, and so are the ornery capsules of *vache sacrée* couchsurfer Freud. My favorite, though, is the book relating the pushpin field battles of atheist and agnostic, as delicately transcribed by war reporter Comte-Sponville. There's something very comforting about the list, like the smell of leather from a new school satchel or the feel of virgin notebooks. Entertained by glimpses into imaginations from centuries elapsed, by fireballs of spirituality's recalcitrant bad boy and rock star Krishnamurti, and by the many despondences of Arjuna, still heartbreaking across time—I fall asleep to these bedrock tunes of worlds so different from mine and to narratives of rituals whose meanings I won't ever fully grasp. I didn't miss being in school, structured by finite terms and expectations of tasks given by others, but I realize I missed learning.

"Rule Three: General duties of a teacher: Pull everything out of your students." From the ten rules edicted for teachers and students by artist and educator Sister Corita Kent, and pollinated by John Cage, I recall the third the next day when the professor inspects my pose.

"Sit bones. Both. Down. Right one too."

What's wrong with my right one?

"Your right sit bone, yes."

He sighs, saying, "You have facility but you lack consciousness," then walks away to mess with the next person.

I lack consciousness!? The sentence worms its way inside my left ear canal and thus, with these three little words, I am shocked into realizing I truly had no idea my two sit bones were behaving differently. I lack consciousness, not flexibility or muscles. My pride is hurt. I don't know about you but that's about the harshest thing anyone could tell me about myself, especially if that anyone is in charge of the training that, despite my ill health, I want to ace so badly.

Well, I'm not surprised. The words find an echo in that mental ravine of mine and now they've piled up over some other tasty words of the same ilk that, years ago, crash landed at the bottom of my pit: inconsistent, unassertive, coquette, spoiled, selfish. I'm ready to believe anything and anyone at this point, so low is my… my consciousness? Even in a yoga class, I feel under the gun to perform, and outperform others. How then could the practice change me? I start doubting I can go deep into myself and reach spiritual plateaus of any sort, no matter the amount of yoga I do. Hours of training, years of practice, and I'm nowhere nearer seeing the light. Yoga moves too slowly for me. I must slow down.

14

BEFORE OUT, THERE'S IN. The intake.

It's a beautiful hypothetical day in a neighborhood devoid of friends, acquaintances, and preferably even passersby. It might be in labyrinthic La Kalsa in Palermo. Been there, done it, got lost in it. Could also be I'm tripping down wet stairs in Montmartre, hotfooting in Hackney. Shadowboxing in Santa Rosa, or the Sassi. Flatlining in Prenzlauer Berg. I got stuck looping there as well. Highland Park, or Gulou. Did done do that there. These neighborhoods, devoid for me of neighbors, I walked them all with the same mad dance steps set to the immutable frenzied rhythm of my perfect hunger pangs, my delicious chemical highs, my blind spots. I walked them all, and wasted them all. Mere backdrops, sceneries—not too shabby either—rented for my own walking orgies.

Indeed, indeed it's a beautiful day to be alive and I am alive, oh yes, I am so very alive at this moment of wanting. See, I am chomping through the fading hour at neck-breaking speed. I am so very, excruciatingly conscious, conscious I am an eating body. It is last month, last week, and yesterday. It could be today, tomorrow, and twenty years ago as well. With each bite of food, I tear into the deathlike numbness that weighs down my footsteps. I am alive, a mad spider on uppers, caught in her own web. The dance, the dance, it wakes me, lifts me, lights me. I'm wanting and wanting more. Fuck need. I scream in cavernous silence. This, my only, my best, and most consistent practice, stickier than yoga, older than singing, more frequent than sex or even smiles, and I rise up to the beat of a heart I hear loudest and clearest in these moments of rapture. Tap, drums, tap. Alive, living, not food, is my drug.

Today, it is the cloudless sun. Yesterday, it might have been a different trigger—dwelling on heartbreak, rubbing in a slight, a stomach upset maybe, plain hunger even, or the onset of menstrual bleeding. No, today, nothing of the sort. It, the episode, would be launching from a place of peace. Imagine on a calm sea, a luxury cruise ship and on its upper deck sunning bodies stretched motionless. I am sea, ferry, and passengers. Even-keeled, I have had a good day. Nothing happened. I haven't wanted. I am content. And I pace, simply walking, simply swishing my blood inside the crucible of my body. This might just be what normal feels like and it is odd, disconcerting: a breeze over the promenade; woolen clouds darkening above. It could be morning, more likely afternoon when the steering due the day is done. It is the eye of the storm. Below the hull, swarms of laughing fish. It is indeed from the deck a beautiful day with unobstructed views of.... Of what?

Nothing disquieting happened today, and I now find me wanting. Wanting for content to anchor me down.

In that shapely and friendless neighborhood, I stand now at a crossroads. I take a left, walk through piazza San Paolo and enter a sunless alley of ancient buildings whose highest floors lean in like a stone tunnel over my steps. I am hitting the pavement harder. There's something military now about the way my heels catch the ground as if I am training for a drill parade. I want so much to believe that today is the start of a new life, that I am fine, from here on fine, please. I plead with myself. Just stop walking now. Step back from the tunnel. Turn around. You said, never again, you said it yesterday, a few hours ago. Don't go there. But I go. I take it apart now but I still don't understand how I snap. At what point do I say, fuck it, I give up?

There I am, though.

Earlier, I bought safe groceries—a box of four organic eggs, sheets of spring roll rice paper, and seaweed. All *bio*. I am being good, so good to myself—a certified over-the-counter health nut. All fine so far, and I'm not ready to go home yet. Keep walking. It's still early, not quite the evening and I've not been out of the house yet today so I'm going to do what I think normal people do and treat myself to a stroll and enjoy it. Is this where it goes awry, at wanting "normal"? What do I really want at this point? I pat myself on the back, tell myself this is a good thing, to walk. I feel safe. I like to think I'm gonna be okay today. I don't want to think about it too much. I don't want to think about anything too much. No more questions, no more choices. Don't want to jinx this. Say it again, this is an enjoyable city and I've chosen myself, chosen to be here. I'm lucky to be here. But what I really want is the high. Fuck "normal."

After the tunnel of walls, I cross through another piazza, walk now along Via Alighieri to the alley that leads to the town cinema. I consider for a minute going in to catch a movie, any movie. I'm treating myself this evening, right? There's a showing in a couple minutes. I'll do that. In a minute. I don't feel rushed. The walk has been leisurely and I enjoy being outside in the late afternoon light, the golden hour as I knew it to be called when I lived in Los Angeles. All is well. I deserve a pleasant evening. I am owed. To be happy. Happy. I can decide that myself, for myself. Being alone sucks. Being alone is great.

I could have stopped there, stopped before snapping. I didn't. Under pressure to have it all, I didn't. I would be sitting in the sweet alternate reality of the theater but this won't happen. I think to treat myself just a bit more—I deserve it, we deserve happiness, don't we? Don't we all? Ah, the weight of the obligation, like smiling at strangers, oh America, smiling—made and kept happy—why not, it's easy—by indulging in a scoop of gelato—such a normal thing, isn't it, ice cream? It's not hunger, not for food at least.

The bartering begins.

There's a gelateria across the street. I walk toward it, telling myself I have eaten enough and eaten well today. I make a deal with myself that I won't eat the entire scoop of ice cream. But if that's the case—let me and myself make a deal—if I won't eat the whole thing, I might as well have real ice cream and not sorbet, the lighter, healthier, kinder option. Yes, yes, I stay away from ice cream for terror of lactose messing up my delicate digestive system. But a lick or two is all I want and need, I think. I'm normal, aren't I?

Ice cream? I'm playing with fire now.

Inside the shop, grasping for countenance—in an Italian shop with my Franchica beatbox, to pass as a wallflower—I zoom in on the list of available flavors. Ahead, in front of me, a fat woman with a crying four-year-old boy in a stroller, orders. Negotiates the scoop be split over two cones so that she can give one to the squirming toddler. Keep cool. Bambino is having a fit of rage now, tossing around in the stroller, trying to break free from his seat. He's loud. Sugar's a serious kiddie drug. Sugar is an atomic any-age drug, but I'm stopping there right now; I can't turn the mirror to me as I stand in line ordering my fix. I'm me now, not that screaming invalid on tiny wheels. Tssss. His mama hands bambino a scoop that the counter girl has graciously, empathically topped with a generous helping of chantilly. We, I, you, all scream for ice cream. Sugar-fixed, kiddie instantly calms down. Meantime, I've decided on pistachio flavor with very dark, melting chocolate. One, si. Small, please. Not over a cone, no. Paper cup. Fewer calories. Small serving, this is so very reasonable, so very European. I pay the one euro sixty and exit frame left.

I cross the street while taking a first quick stab at the pistachio—start there, start mild. It tastes decent, just okay, boring, no danger. Lick left, oh, oh glory, decadence, and sulfur! Freaking, mind-blowing chocolate!

Right then and right there, my brain switches to panic mode. It's over. This, people, is where the tipping point resides. This lick, this choco bit, is where the high kicks in. I'm exalting there, and that's it. There is a before and then, this, this tight, step-by-step descent into automatic pilot, hyperawareness, and flushed neurons. I will know every second of every minute of this bubbly bath of brain-teasing molecules.

To begin, I breathe harder. My chest tightens. I still fight it for a very short while and tell myself, hopeful once more, that I will have just one last, final lick of the plastic spoon. As I walk under the building through the passageway that leads to the alley, I've bartered that spoonful into half a cup. There's no one near me in the alley, but I see people standing on the other end of the tunnel on the sidewalk. I think for a second that they are staring at me, and that they are whispering. I back away a few steps but, paranoid still, I know they must be commenting to each other on how oddly I am behaving. They must be. To my left is the entrance to the movie theater, with the cashier standing outside, smoking a cigarette. He feels as removed as a character on screen.

I turn around and face the passageway again. I feel trapped. By now, I'm done thinking I will have just half the cup. The chocolate is gone and I'm eating the pistachio. What if I leave just a spoonful of it? Will that be enough to prove that I was in control and that I won't need anything else and can just go quietly—and victoriously—into the theater, no matter that the show might have started a few minutes ago? But my heart has been loudly thumping from the very moment I first licked the chocolate. Pistachio gone too. Something has clicked in my brain. Sweating and breathing faster, I'm fucked.

Deal? Draw the line at puking? After all, I've made myself a solemn promise not to do it anymore, a heartfelt pledge to get better.

I leave the theater behind, walk back to the main street. I know exactly where I'm going. The map of the city is stored away in my head, dotted with coordinates of those establishments that will provide me with the fast, cheap, and greasy. There, I am walking into one of those places—one of those!—the closest thing to a fast-food joint in this Italian town of matter-of-fact gastronomy. A couple of tables set up on the sidewalk, a half-dozen people ordering their takeaway meals. I wait for my turn, high-strung inside, confident on the outside. A character, as removed from the truth as a screen projection. I've entered the zone from which I can calmly, coolly order whatever the hell I want to order from the offerings behind the glass display. Piadina, piadina, and piadina. Rolled-up or folded, with meats and mozzarella, hints of lettuce-green and tomato-red. Focaccia, hefty bread triangles plus a dash of sauce without cheese. The same bread triangles again but this time with translucent slices of potatoes but no tomato. I point at the two closest to me. One has ham, I can see, and I like. The other one, a folded pocket covered with small breadcrumbs, is a mystery at this point. I ask the guy in my uncertain Italian and with much gesturing not to heat them up, that I'll take them away as they are. He wraps them up, adds napkins to the bag, and hands me the lot. I don't remember how much it was. I remember getting a large smile and enjoying giving a smile back, but I can feel the back of my head already turned around and pulling me back and away into the street. Half of my body wants to stay and linger here in the shop, watch people and the movements of fingers and eyes, money being exchanged and words spoken and heard. That part of me that loves the human stories is sitting down at the sidewalk table with its tall, built-in metal stool, and is unwrapping the package leisurely. To be sitting next to a family of two or four! The kids are eating in peace while staring at the traffic. The parents are dabbing a cheek, taking a bite, looking at each other. I'm under a large tree, the cars arrive from two different directions and take turns merging into the main street, a mechanical ballet. There is a sign that reads Potenza. The temperature is perfect.

And there is that other part of me that's focusing hard and fast on the food displayed, the me that's figured out her exit strategy and assessed every single person in the shop for their potential to see through the routine being performed here. Which one of these people will look at me and understand what I'm doing? I don't look normal. I'm tense. Everyone else looks pretty relaxed. Which one will want more from me than I can give? Which one will talk to me? Want to connect? They must want it, why wouldn't they? Approach and see through me? I'm taking the package, putting back my change in my favorite, fur-coated coin purse, the one that looks like a dead cat. I'm taking a step back toward the exit. I'm still acting very cool and composed, yet I move energetically enough that it really looks like I've got somewhere to go and can't be bothered. I think I look absolutely abnormal, like a robot. I am on the sidewalk. I brush aside a kid, two kids, walk past a dog on a leash and a few couples lingering, waiting for their paper-wrapped grease fests. I leave the scene, my package in hand. I know there is a side street a few steps away. I take it, the noise of the main street subsides a bit.

Single-minded, on my track, I walk, walk fast enough that I can't be next to someone long enough for them to question what I'm doing, the old car at the red light trick. Human being pulls up next to you at the red light, stops car. Let them think they can turn their head and get a glimpse of you, human too, on the line. But then, back up your car just a few feet, disappear from their sight, protected. Safety measures. Be gone from sight and the company of humans. Red light obscurity. I am no one then. Not a singer, not a woman, not this nor that, not anything but this back-up motion. Or so I think. On foot, this is what it sounds like. I am on the left sidewalk, cross over to the right sidewalk to keep ahead of oncoming pedestrians on the left sidewalk. What asininity. There is a woman holding a kid by the hand. They're walking alongside, going in the same direction as I am but on the other sidewalk. I hear her say a few words to the kid, words I don't understand. I wonder if she's noticed me, and if she has, what she is seeing. I let them pass, slowing down. She's pulling the kid along. They're indissociable. I'm elsewhere. Wrapping paper ripped, my heart is racing. I'm sweating. Throat is clinching. Lips tighten. I'm breathing faster. I'm walking faster. And yet I'm keeping it all cool from the darker side of this two-way mirror. I see an opaque surface of water barely registering the slight breeze above. The winds pick up. I am still wrinkle-free, unperturbed. Right hand through the paper folds, I grab the first of two blobs, the one with ham and cheese. From the bottom of the festering lake, thick with grabby weeds and tangled roots, there emerges a cryptid. I eat the ham and cheese conglomerate in the street while walking. I do not pause, and I'm done chomping it all down by the time I get to the next intersection, bite after big bite and swallowing whole. I notice crumbs on my shirt, I wipe them out and they resist. I clean my greasy fingers on my pants. I pull out the second wrapped piadina, the pièce de résistance, leaky, heavy, and warm in my left hand as I turn right onto the next street. I take a few steps while uncovering it and chomp on the top corner of the piadina along with some wrapping paper. This one confection is a study in off-whites, gooey texture of béchamel-filled dough and melted mozzarella layers. Interesting. I've never tried anything like it before. As far as street food is concerned, it's a five or six out of ten – a bit impractical, especially if it's still warm and drippy, and this one I'm holding is bordering on being hot. I have to sit down for a minute or this is going to get messy. I spot an isolated ledge above some stairs and sit. I'm just behind a telephone pole and a parked van. I ask myself if this is a safe spot, a place where I can rightfully pretend to eat something without seeming out of place.

I finish the food, brush off the bits that fell on my shirt, on my lap.

I rub my face, lick my mouth clean.

This whole thing might have taken one minute. I eat fast, it's a given.

I get up, throw the paper bag and napkins in the trashcan. There's always a convenient trash bin. I like perching next to them and knowing where my things are thrown away and how well they'll keep away.

I start walking again, wondering if I should go for more of the same, in a different place of course. I quickly run through the lay of the town in my head, remembering the places I've seen that sell take-out food. I think of the grocery stores, assess the time it would take me to go through the aisles, pick what I need and make it home to eat. Grocery spoils are not all street-ready. Milk, cereal, breads require a sit-down, utensils. Plus I don't want to go for a full-blown feed. I think of the Focacceria on the main street, pedestrian at this hour.

I enter the main piazza, take a look at the people strolling with family or friends, dressed up nice and convivial.

I make it to the Focacceria, a couple of people ahead of

me. I imagine the transaction will be simple and fairly fast. It won't get too cumbersome. In this shop I almost know how to ask for what I want in Italian. I have loose change. I am the consummate consumer. No questions asked, no bargaining, just buy and get out. I always leave with something and don't return items. The well-oiled cog in a well-cogged machine.

"Francese?"

Si.

"Parigi?"

Si.

"Grazie."

Prego.

"Ciao."

Buona sera.

I take home a bag of cookie-like bread confections. I don't know their name, those beige wheat dry bite-size maybe anise-flavored mini bagel-shaped crunchy taralli, but I'm glad when I spot them on the shelf, like the face of an old friend at the dentist's. I recall how they so sweetly and swiftly dissolve in liquids, be it flavored milk or will-have-to-do-tonight water, and having so elegantly become liquefied, how painless their extraction back up becomes. The hands on my clock point to images and not numbers. The first is a lemon cake, the last a box of chocolates. The moving hands don't stop. Cake gives way to crackers, and crackers inexorably to milk, milk to cornflakes, gnocchi straight from the bottom, followed by chocolate bar, hotdog sausage, cookie dough, moldy peanuts and expired vanilla yogurt and olives with pits. I make instantaneous decisions. If I see it, I eat it. It's all good.

But yes, I am walking at a normal pace still and I eat

through the second focaccia before I get to the Duomo, the cathedral. I keep walking past, not stopping to take in the view to the old city, and I walk under ancient arches. There, I rip open the bag of the dry bread cookies. I eat one after the other, taking care to salivate enough so that the mass won't obstruct my esophagus when I puke it back out. I walk by my old neighborhood buddy, the silent retired man who sits on his chair at sundown in front of his apartment. I speed up my pace, sure don't want to acknowledge him today. Can't. So I diss him. And yes, those are the sorts of unfriendly signals people pick up well here. Like animals in a herd. You are nice, you are not, but you can't go back and forth. You want to be left alone or you want to lead the pack. It's all clear, and politely, people adjust their expectations and dip back inside their shells.

At last, after one more turn and one more turn, and fifty stairs, I make it home with just one last acknowledgment of social niceties when I nod to the couple of tourists whose path I cross as I'm about to go through my door. Was that a nod with a hint of a seductive wink maybe? Me tourist, you tourists, so let's make nice. Something like an acknowledgment of presence, maybe the whiff of scent recognition from one tourist to the other. None of us is from here but we eat up locales. We are just passing a few hours in a place and time not of our own. But me, when I'm in the busy of a crisis, I'm in my haunts, charted territory. Few things, nothing, can derail me from my single-minded purpose, to feel that high and to get through to the other side of the crisis. And tourist I remain, on the outskirts of the day, following the signs to this and that sight, and clocking in the numbered stops along the way. Just follow the signs to the church of redemption and the fountain of original sins.

Don't tip your guide. She's just doing her job.

★ ★ ★

Are you bored yet? Because I am. I am deeply, happily, tragically bored. Once I have boarded the food truck or slid onto the puke track, walked into the garden of delirious delights and hitched the high cart, there's not much else there than what has already happened countless times in the same ways and manners for the past twenty years.

Twenty years?

A kid with a nightmare. I've had that same nightmarish vision visit me ever since I've been small, just old enough to know I was haunted. I'd wake up every night from the same terrifying scene. There's a very pleasant garden under the sun, on one end of a dark tunnel made of giant truck tires. In that garden, white plastic chairs are set around a white outdoor table. It's all looking very summery, with vibrant, edible greens and husked yellows, flowers maybe. Yet, it's a nightmare. To go through that dark passage, the tunnel, slimy and rubbery. To be that darkness and then to be that light, and yet to feel this is all a mistake and what do I care about a bright garden since the tunnel won't let me through.

No, not much else happens. I don't sit at the garden table. I don't throw the chairs. No one else comes out of the living, breathing, constricting tunnel. No, I'm the only child and birth is a dreadful, deadly garden party.

* * *

I'm in the kitchen.

I've laid out the food, taken out whatever bowl and plate and spoon and knife I'm going to be needing. The cookie bag is open with what's left of the cookies in it. I've locked the door. The curtains are drawn. There's water in the coffee cup. I don't have milk today so water will do to soften the cookies. Wisely—sadly, I've not been stocking anything in the kitchen that I might want to use up in a blast-off. No milk, no cream, butter, no chocolate cake, no sweets of any sorts, this is health-food central, a pantry from the dire days. All the food I eat under the "normal" guise is just no fun to have around for a bingeria. Green beans, red peppers, half of a cabbage, half a bottle of wine that's been in the fridge for three weeks. Three eggs and moldy tomato sauce in a glass jar. Half a peach, also turned bad. On a shelf next to the sink, there is rice, some brown, some black, some wild, all three organic. Flours of amaranth, brown rice, buckwheat, and chestnut. Ground flax seed. Teas, coffees.

I check for signs of glucose running through my veins already, that excited feel of sugar rushing to the brain. I watch for signs of lactose making its way through my digestive track. I don't feel discomfort but rather a fullness that's not disagreeable yet, as if I'd just had a good meal, not too heavy and not too light. The glucose from the ice cream is the first to take a stand in my blood. I'm slightly joyful and with an energy that comes from the glucose's timed release. You gotta give it to the Italian gelato. It's not junk food by any means.

Let me food-curate for you, critique the offerings here.

As with all the dishes I've had here in my short stay in Italy, the ice cream is well balanced in taste and textures, a refined interplay of fat and sugar, colors and shapes – even the amount a perfected delicacy. I wonder what color it will come out when I puke it—last to splash back up as it was the first thing I ingested? Actually, I stop wondering while I'm busy finishing off the last of the cookies. I don't know if I have that stupid grin of ecstasy on my face or the tight jaw of a stress monster, eyes darting around like a trapped rabbit. It's a pragmatic question. Am I drinking enough liquid? Is this food too compact and heavy that it risks sinking to the bottom of my esophagus and might not come back out? Can I keep going with one more cake or are the calories of the first foods I ate thirty minutes, an hour ago already making their way into my body and making me fat? Will I come out thinner or will I be bloated tomorrow? Will I be feeling stable enough to not want to do this again tomorrow?

That's about it. In no time, I'll have the kitchen cleared and its counter surfaces cleaned up of crumbs and oily skid marks. Junk food purged, down-the-drained, and plastic wrappers binned, this zero-defect kitchen once again proof to the unsuspecting mind that I'm a paragon of healthy eating, a most pristine and pure figment.

I'm in the bathroom now.

I lift the lid of the toilet bowl.

15

NEXT DAY, THE PROFESSOR obliquely asks what I will be doing, where I'll be going after the training. I spill out my litany: Italy, Palermo. Not Paris, no way. Was in Tucson, Seattle, now here, an asinine triptych but not staying, no. Why does he want to know? I could ask him but I'm afraid to find out. When I get home, I spend what's left of the day on the couch. Empty, I'm empty at last. My arms are heavy, my legs sore. But wait, that's not true. I get up and take Cat out to the enclosed garden in the courtyard down below our balcony. Plants, leaves, earth. Cat gets to experience green things for a few minutes, and I do too. Mush, smells, grass to chew and spit. In that sliver of nature, with some sunflowers, a few bushes and a couple of tall trees, everything is just as well as it should be. I'm as well as I can be for the time being. Alone, undisturbed, without calls or visits from anyone. My parents? We rarely speak, and when we do, triangulated, no matter the combination I get on the other end of the line—mom/daughter, dad/daughter or more likely mom/dad/daughter with mom doing all the talking, dad silent in the background and daughter fretting—the conversation never lasts very long. The more infrequent the calls, the less pleasant they are. Emails are one-liners at best about practical matters—the maintenance of the gas heater or the building's annual owners' meeting. When did we stop having anything to say to one another? When did we ever?

My mother was in her teens, perhaps fifteen or sixteen, when her only sister, older by a few years, died from sepsis in the days after giving birth. I knew that much about my family and it was scant. Maybe as a result of that loss, my mother went on to train as a nurse. Fears, phobias, and hatred like so many booby traps, get handed down from one generation to the next. Being her first-formed, did I catch her apprehension of childbearing like a virus through the bloodstream? Nursing school must have promised an escape from her small village, with the prospect of a job in town or even elsewhere in the country. What I do know is that she was angry, not only at the death of her sister but at her family's—especially her own mother's—lack of acknowledgment that she too, the young sister, was suffering from the loss. All her life, she held on to the belief—and the pain—that she had been neglected, passed over as the second-born, a less feminine, less valuable version of the deceased daughter. Born in a farming family in southwestern France, with a traditional upbringing that mandated a family's wealth be handed down to the first-born, my mother must have quickly understood she had to make her mark elsewhere.

She found herself a husband with good prospects, the valedictorian of his engineering school and a man maybe just as uneasy with his upbringing—or his self—as she was. He liked to describe himself as a bumpkin. Both eager to escape where they came from, these two were ripe for emigration. It took them fifteen years after the birth of their first child but they made it to America, by then a family of five. My first brother was born a couple of years after me, and five years after him, the third child, a second son, came along. Thing is, the past has a way of sneaking on board the ocean liner and hiding in the bilges. In America, my brothers and I found ourselves in tight quarters with two people who had gotten everything they had ever dreamed of. For him, a job at the top of the ladder with a salary to match in a "Tie-less Fridays" work environment, and children who had been pushed to excel at school from birth—and had been excelling—given the incredible chance to experience a new country. For her? A distance of six thousand miles from her village maybe, and a chance to prove herself—I grew up hearing legendary tales of *oncles d'Amérique*, the late 19th century emigrants to Latin America, "uncles" who returned to their villages in Béarn and Pays Basque loaded with Venezuelan gold. America was going to be amazing. It would keep the family together. It would give the children the world. Six months into our new life in Arizona, I was slowly killing myself, and my younger brother's beautiful face was entirely covered with puberty zits like I've never seen on anyone before. Brother #1 seemed to be the only one who had it together. Maybe because middle children are good at making—and keeping—friends, he didn't seem to be visibly afflicted by our new life.

★ ★ ★

The time has come to say goodbye. "One, two and... cheese." The secretary, the skinny girl, the bald guy, and the older woman from the back row, the one with long tresses, the big girl who manages the best handstands, the actress who's always late to class.... We strike our last pose of the training, huddled giggling around *le prof*, standing stiff and still for our class photo. Forty-three faces, not counting those who dropped off mid-course. Of those faces, I know a dozen names at most. In a few weeks, I'll have forgotten all but two or three. Month is over, hear, hear. Hold it—smile. Now, everyone, breathe out.

Class photos. In their yellowed cardboard frames, my French school pictures have been kept boxed up, shelved, and triaged not by me—I never took the time, who ever takes the time at twenty, thirty, forty even to go through their old school photos?—but by my mother when, retired, reflective, and redundant, she began sorting through our lives—never admittedly hers. In the Marianne corner of my parents' large and well-organized attic—one corner mine, a corner for each brother, and everything else my parents'—there are boxes, bags, and pyramids, bursaries of five lifetimes.

I've only ever sought out the photos of us children in brusque rows when a more curious or ingrained lover gets to asking what it was like, what I was like back then, back when I was a French schoolgirl of six, ten, fifteen. What I was like? I don't know. I remember skipping cafeteria lunches so I could spend that time by myself with my young thoughts in an empty classroom where I'd attempt to write poetry and would peer from high windows into the courtyard of post-lunch affairs for inspiration. It was a typical French high school from the 1980s, with no hardback yearbooks to buy and no souvenir shop or vending machines. No press club or school paper, no drama team or pledges at the basketball games for that matter. What there was, though, as there would be in Arizona, was a class photo op each year.

My yoga graduation? For the first time in my life, I'm in step with my class. I'm graduating with everyone else. It's a big deal, the first time I have stuck around to receive a diploma. It didn't happen with high school in France—I left for America, managed to get the French *baccalauréat* degree by studying on my own at home—or in the States. With my French degree, I was able to skip straight to college after only half a year of high school, a teaser meant more to socialize than educate me. It didn't happen with college either. After four years, I remained one class short of fulfilling the requirements for my BA in film production—a semester of chemistry away from the piece of paper. Piece of paper too, my marriage license, the easiest, fastest path to the green card that would allow my husband to remain in the States. We, fashionable, thought wedding vows out of style. We divorced ten years later in a misguided attempt to save our relationship by first removing the weight of the administrative sentence. Although our logic wasn't as flawed as it sounds, divorcing still didn't do the trick. Next, we tried living in separate houses, but then eventually separated. Both divorce and marriage proceedings were unceremonious affairs, with officiating clerks bemused at my nonchalance. It seemed to hurt less if I denied their importance to the obligatory rites of passage. Marriage, graduation, wrinkles and night cream. Maybe I wasn't cut out for any of it. Always out of step, one stop removed, voluntarily or involuntarily segregated, I must have liked doing things my way. Did I ever get caught caring?

The French class photos would have been taken outdoors under one of the old chestnut trees while the fall weather was still good enough. Thirty to forty kids whose names I've long forgotten. Why would I have remembered? I had moved on far, far away. Switched to high school in the suburban desert of Arizona. There, we were photographed as individuals. One smiling mug shot among hundreds of others—a profitable business for the photographer. Lining in alphabetical order the pages of the yearbook, we sported '80s bouffant hairdos and straightening braces, waxed crew cuts, and cowboy shirts, a whole age group grinning from the bleachers of the popularity-contest bible. If you were liked well enough, your own book would be filled with cute comments and perky side jokes, courtesy of your upbeat classmates. My brother, always the jokester, had managed to get himself in twice, showing up for both the junior and the senior photo roll call.

I don't have any portraits from the college years that followed. I was making movies and pasting street art protest posters around campus. Obsessed with making a mark in the Los Angeles indie film scene, I had no time for class photos or prom outings, friends, homecomings, cheerleading, or hand-holding. My boyfriend at the time was also my filmmaking partner. He was the most talented of our class, as much the valedictorian as my father had been in his own school. That fact didn't strike me until years later, and I never questioned while living and working with him why I needed to stand behind my man, and not the reverse. I was a hardworking, unassuming, and shy girl. It would be a long time before I understood the dire consequences of that strategy for my sense of self-worth. Keeping my side of the bargain by giving full support to husband, boyfriend, male bandmates, and lovers, I simply did what I had been taught was normal.

So today, I want my yoga photo and I want to rejoice. This moment is mine. I exchange numbers with the other musician in our class. Could I help her scheme some new songs, she slyly asks? I wave to my floor neighbor and the gazelle smiles back with a promise to meet soon, next week maybe at a café. Everyone is smiling, smiling at me, and I smile back. I'm now certified to teach yoga, with a piece of paper to prove it. However I stack it—Yoga Alliance-recognized, 200RYS, Hatha/Yin-abled—I've done it. Now do I frame the certificate, string it around my neck and move on to something completely different? It's late June and I'm in Paris on a tight leash of my own making. I've bought myself some time by staying put for a month but it's been my plan from the time I left Tucson to hightail it back to Palermo as soon as possible after training. Soon, I'd be hiding out with Cat in some statuesque palace, licking my wounds and pecking at my marbled flesh while practicing bending over—the toilet bowl, all white flecks in my field of vision—as only a flexible—and certified—yogini can.

Is that it? What a plan. I'd rather not think about it.

In the courtyard over Tupperware lunches, plans are being made to keep in touch. With just a few days before my flight, I would love to do something different and throw a party, as I would have done in Tucson under similar circumstances. See, I've gotten used to these people, my everyday floormates and I want to let them know I appreciated the company. Maybe we'll all make friends for life. We are a community, right? Kindred, we've all been altered by the training, haven't we? Yoga matters to us. Maybe we can discuss it for a change, and, over petit-fours, ask of ourselves, what did we get out of it? Did it change our lives? Are we better people? As I pass the dark chocolate tablet around, I speak up with the offer to host a cocktail party at my apartment. Helen, Stéphanie, Silvia… yes, they'll all be there. What a wonderful idea. We must keep in touch. This has been such a wonderful, life-changing month. We will never forget. The American mother says she'll start a Facebook page. We will keep in touch.

⋆ ⋆ ⋆

I was ten, ahead one grade and one year younger than my classmates, when I started *collège*, junior high school in France. A quiet, brainy student, I had been plucked from our small, combined grades village classroom and slipped up one notch ahead of my time to the big school in the next town. Until then, I had walked mornings and afternoons, no more than ten minutes away by mini hops, to and from our small school with my kid brother in tow, leather satchels strapped over our shoulders, two good little foot soldiers hungry for their future. We walked by the old medieval church where, with children my age, I'd soon be having my first communion in the spring—a graduation of sorts, yes, and one I was glad to forget. We walked by the café stocked with bread, cigarettes, and the candy bars we stole every Friday afternoon from under the shopkeeper's nose on our way to weekly catechesis. Sometimes, our timing coinciding with theirs, we'd walk alongside other kids who'd popped out from one of the big new houses, some with swimming pools, that had been erected over the fields where brown cows once roamed, grazing and trickling fat milk into pink udders that dragged low between their muddy hind legs. And, if their bus was running on time, as we got to the last crossroad, the one with the old stinky farm, we'd wave toward the big kids inside, the ones who, until just a few months before, had been fixtures of our school playground, now shuttled to another reality, that of the big school in the next town.

A year later, I was in that school bus, waving goodbye to the kids my age—my schoolmates no more. I was taken past the church, the sweets café, beyond the Green Giant corn fields that sprawled where the Roman encampment had once stood—or so swore the old farmer who lived next to our house who would hand me smooth shards of pottery that, once polished, looked really, really ancient, and most certainly were to this child's imagination. I was on my own now in the big school to make new friends while keeping up the good grades.

⋆ ⋆ ⋆

The yoga training is over and I am sad the next day, at a loss for something to do—but I remember that in a couple of days I will see everyone again here in my kitchen. After I introduce them to Cat and feed everyone, I won't feel so lonely. The morning of the get-together, my cocktail initiative, I am up early to bake and cook. Let's get personal, my fellow Parisians. I expect that quite a few people will come. The whole class and *le prof* have received the perky e-fliers I designed with date, time, metro directions, address, and access code plus landline number. I get some polite thanks by return email, with a few polite promises to show up.

"Can we bring the kids?" asks the blonde German mom.

Of course.

"How late will it run?" inquires the trainer from Marseille, always on schedule. Depends. All night if need be.

"Do we need to bring anything?"

No, no worries, I say to the Montmartre barmaid. I'll take care of it all. Just come. Be my guests. Come! Bring yourselves, your kids, and boy toys. It's an afternoon tea, an apéritif, a drinking binge, whatever you want it to be but I can't let you all go now, my friends, without saying goodbye.

★ ★ ★

Eight in the morning. The shops open in an hour. I need to make food, but what food? What do my yoga mates like to eat? All month long, I noticed lunches of rice and tofu, baguette cheese sandwiches, and *petits sablés* cookies washed down with green tea—Kombucha for the most up-to-date ones. I'll make my party favorite, the vegan potato salad with dill, and quiches and cakes, maybe even bake some chocolate chip cookies.

I stock up on juices and cheese, breads and veggies. I must have shopped for fifty. Tidied up the apartment too. No more suspicious speckles of food on the walls around the toilet, the place looks clean and inviting, and even smells pretty good. I brushed Cat. She now inspects the kitchen as I get down to spreading fun tidbits on many good crackers, to uncorking sweet wines and to layering nibbles of complementary colors that swirl in the nice bowls I found, neglected, in the cabinetry. Only thing missing are red balloons and party favors. And people.

★ ★ ★

Schoolwork I liked well enough as a child. English, a new subject when I went to *collège* at ten, was a favorite. Homework kept me head-down occupied, if not wholly invested, but my parents started getting rightfully concerned that I was putting good grades over social interactions and, for the afternoon of my eleventh birthday, invited on my behalf a dozen kids to the party they wanted me to want and thought I needed. I didn't have to lift a finger. I rarely did. These things just seemed to happen for my own sake. Not only were there kids, some from the old school and some from my current one, but there were gifts galore, party favors for everyone. My mom had gone out of her way to buy presents not just for me but for her/my guests too. Out in the yard, we played the games she'd chosen and the kids won colored pencils, butterfly clips, and strawberry-smelling erasers. An hour into it, one of the girls turned to me in disbelief.

"Is this *your* birthday or *our* birthday?" she asked. "We're getting all these things. It's weird."

I blushed, becoming self-conscious that friends were being bought for me. This was wrong. I hadn't asked for any help. My parents were so anxious to see me perform well that they took to doing some of my schoolwork for me. The first week of *collège*, my father made an architect-grade tent card from thick cardboard, something that I, at that age, would have been unable to make. The next day, the arts and craft teacher who had requested the namecard, our first assignment, dismissed the fake.

"Not your own work, not worth anything. Learn to do things by yourself. This is crap."

Again, I blushed. This teacher had seen through me, his shrug cutting through the little lie that propped me up as a good student. I didn't forget his response and didn't know there would be more like it for years to come—and that I would seek them out. I was suffocating from my parents' over-involvement in my life but had no words to say it. A couple of years later, I got out of the bus one morning and walked toward the gray school building, feeling funny in my stomach. As I got to the gate, I threw up my breakfast on the asphalt. I felt neither shame nor guilt at that instant. I wasn't hiding and didn't feel self-conscious. All that day at my desk, I found the stench from my stained shoes oddly comforting. It was proof that I had been sick when my schoolmates had not, and made me feel apart and different from them. Alone too, as if I had left everyone else behind and escaped the doldrums of school days for an uncharted journey. Yes, I was bored on school grounds. In a stroke of luck, bile and asphalt became the two improbable flint stones that sparked a bit of self-awareness that day. I had stumbled upon a way to vanish in my mind and still remain, by all appearances, a high-performing student on the chair where she belonged, the good daughter who would not ever openly cause her parents to worry.

★ ★ ★

Four o'clock, all is set for the arrival of my yoga buddies. I'm sitting on the balcony, brushing and combing Cat again, and waiting for my friends. It's a really nice June day. Cat tires of my yanking at her fur. She goes in the kitchen and eyes the wieners. I water the plants. We wait and wait all afternoon.

By dusk, I give up.

No one, no one showed up. Zero. Not a single person from the studio. Not one text message to say we're late, we'll be there, or simply, sorry to miss the fun. I am in the kitchen, surrounded by more food than I can fit back in the fridge. What was I thinking? I got this place all wrong. Ain't Dodge no more, that's for sure. French people are odd. What did I do wrong? Cakes first. I will go back to Palermo with Cat, just as planned. Paris, it's not you, it's me. I'm just not into you. Cookies next. I don't care that no one came. I won't share. My food. Crackers. Dips. Chips. I speed-chew through the feast—my food. I made it. I own it. Swallow all, puke it all. I don't care. That no one came.

★ ★ ★

Later that evening, sunk numb over the computer, I cringe when I see the group photo pop up on the Facebook page for our class. There I am in the first row, looking stiff as a statue. Stretched thin and stern with a puffed chest, a caricature of the spiritual warrior, I look like some sort of bad joke on serenity. At least I'm not showing teeth with my smile, unlike some of the other happy babies in the photo who fly their grins full-mast. I bench my Mona Lisa half moon crescent but what those dark-sunken, transfixed eyes betray is simply desperation, looking straight into the lens in a learned and practiced form of immobility that could pass as spirituality or stand in for wisdom in this castle of cards.

Could be worse, says the wise man, but I breathe shallowly, paralyzed in the stasis of a fragile ceasefire with my bad habits and eluding the question of what the others thought of me during our time together. The sharp anxiety shows, to my eyes at least, in this tight-lipped portrait now online. True fact: I sit frozen in fear of being found out, with the intuition that the roof is about to fall over my head. I'd seen that look before on earthquake-shaken people in New Zealand. I had reached Christchurch in the southern island a couple of weeks after a major earthquake. My scheduled show had been canceled—the venue had collapsed—but I went to the ravaged town anyway and offered to play a fundraiser for the local radio station. There, I met survivors who had had little choice but—or were stubborn enough—to remain sleeping in their cracked houses through weeks of aftershock tremors. They had the bearing of people whose roof might at any time collapse and bury them alive. Who would want to come over to my cocktail party and stick around? Who wouldn't get uncomfortable looking into those eyes?

16

A MONTH AFTER SPACE shuttle Challenger lit up the Florida sky, on that morning of January 1986 when, sitting at our high school desks in Phoenix, we bowed our heads in a stunned minute of silence through which echoed her mighty blast, I started holding off on food. I was going to make sure I wasn't built for the launch from childhood. I was sixteen.

It all started with a date, my first ever in the strict American definition of the term. A nice boy had asked me out. He was sweet, smart, and my size. Back where I came from, provincial France, we didn't "date." We hung out—wiggled and slow-danced at *boums*, informally moved in packs and went ten kids to a movie, sheltered from formality by numbers. Not that we weren't little French flirts, deep-tonguing in buses and school hallways, but although the English word "date" sounds plainly *français*—"*une date*" being a date on a calendar page in both languages—I didn't have the equivalent word in my teenage jargon. Was it *sortir ensemble*, to go out together? Was a date meant as courtship appointment, a promise made to kiss—*un flirt avec toi*—or simply a way of showing off your suitability with a burger or liquor drench? It all seemed so serious and regimented. What was that about being picked up at home, and the boy introduced to parents who would be expected to check both his trustworthiness and that of his car brakes? Yes, the outing—oftentimes garnished with a corsage brought by the gent—had to be not just approved but blessed.

And safe. Paranoia was rampant in the 1980s Phoenix suburbia, cancerous monster-in-the-making of a megalopolis. Many of my schoolmates had recently moved to Arizona from out of state and were still settling in. Those like me who came from overseas were still figuring out whose wide, white, and trigger-ready American smile could be trusted. Arizona fathers—mothers too—carried loaded guns and sported Mormon bibles. I didn't quite know what to make of our neighbors. The kids had been equipped from an early age with all sorts of wicked and expensive accessories, growing up fast and fucked-up, derailed mini-adults in beefed-up cars, furious on legal and not-so-legal drugs, sugar, guns, and earlyish sex, with mall jobs to buy mall things and the directionless rage to waste it all. Was I to join in this tribe of flappable desert munchkins, foraging around artificial lakes accessorized with lame ducks and palm trees imported from Mexico? Dates were not the most dangerous thing about this desert mirage of a town, nor were the cars in the hands of electric sixteen-year-olds. There was the 110+ degree summer heat. But even the heat—blamed for a pale, flat-chested willow of a girl fainting in the school's parking lot one morning—was not our worst enemy. It all looked so benign and safe around us, with no street walkers, no homeless people, no trash on the streets and manicured lawn after manicured lawn. Boredom, not heat, was the killer, inflicting a vague but very real sense of imprisonment. That skinny girl who had fainted in the heat? I had noticed her at school. She was sick—like me, but sicker—and her breath smelled of bubble gum. I didn't know then that this fruity smell was a symptom of advanced anorexia. The body eats itself, attacks its muscle mass once all fat is gone, and decomposes from within. As I looked at her lying unconscious next to a new Impala, I wrinkled my nose and moved on. What good could I do her? This didn't concern me, I thought.

* * *

I was on my first date, not yet diseased. We had gone to a football game, possibly between our two teams—we were from different schools, and there were kids from both his and mine tiered in rows on the stadium bleachers. I stood shyly beside my date. We remained, for a long while, at the bottom of the bleachers, a locus of interest, as I understood when a girl I knew only a little pulled me aside and, whispering, asked excitedly if I was dating him. She and her girlfriends were curious. Were we? I didn't know what to say—contradict her?—and got uncomfortably self-conscious. There was no stopping her and her friends. They would keep talking about me. They would judge my looks and assess our moves. It must have been obvious to them that I didn't have a clue how to behave on a date. Was I expected to kiss the boy? Should he be holding my hand? Did I like him? Did I even want to be kissed? Now that I had been exposed as an idiot novice—or, more disturbingly, a desiring being?—I knew I wanted to disappear. Or to become impenetrable.

The next day, I turned down breakfast, had a salad for lunch then said no to steak at dinner. I had embarked on a diet.

Except it wasn't just a diet that I followed through the first spring and summer of my life in America.

* * *

Amenorrhea. It wasn't until four months later while we were back in France for the summer holidays that, in response to my new condition, anorexia, by then alarming, I got scheduled by my mother for the first—and only—doctor's visit that would, if only obliquely, address the subject of my eating disorder. Periods. Their absence—the one clear-cut symptom of the disease that had prompted my mother to act decisively at last—didn't concern me in the least. I didn't bleed, period, but certainly didn't feel I needed help for that, perfectly content to remain in my room and, under my covers at night, study pictures of Fakir Musafar, the San Francisco body-modification performance artist with the otherworldly cinched waist. The words anorexia nervosa had not been uttered nor would they ever be, to me at least, by my parents. The appointment—with someone who spoke her language—was her idea. Not a family doctor, not a therapist but a gynecologist. Had she looked for a specialist? Were there even specialists on eating disorders back then? Anywhere near our French hometown? Were there in Arizona? The topic wasn't in the news and information about treatments must have been scant. No hotlines, no parental guides to be ordered online—no internet.

Fingering around my uterus, the French gynecologist concluded that all down there was as normal as could be expected. My health may have been at risk from severely restricting my intake of calories but the plumbing was still technically sound. Yes, I would bleed again. I would be able to reproduce. There was nothing to worry about. This was just an adolescent phase.

Laidback as the doctor's attitude was, it must have comforted my mother. With her due diligence done, she let me be for the rest of the summer. I was getting mixed signals. If, on one hand, I thought it odd that I should be brought to consult a gynecologist, was I to understand that the trouble with me was that I was growing into a sexual being, into a woman? On the other, I didn't question her leaving me mostly on my own that summer to explore my seventeen-year old self. My budding adventures? Kissing a German boy on the beach in Biarritz and a French man twice my age in the old town center of Toulouse. It was also in that city that, one beautiful afternoon toward the end of the holidays, utterly exhausted, cold, and alone, I curled up on a bench outside the Saint-Sernin basilica and fell asleep. I had been a hardcore anorexic for six months and wasn't any closer to feeling invincible, invisible, or like a woman.

★ ★ ★

It wasn't all a wasted fuck-up of a cloistered, sunless half year. Good little chubby angel no more and dropping fast down through the hatch, those were formative days. Baffled-and-battered-me remembers some pleasurable things not related to food. There was the mosh-pit at a Husker Dü concert, and watching rented movies on the family's newly acquired VHS player, still a novelty in France at the time, but a household essential in our new position as well-off suburbanites in America. I discovered *A Clockwork Orange*—and decided on the spot, marveling at the artfulness of the very first frame of the villa break-in scene, that I would become a film director. I was excited to receive the videotapes of *L'Âge d'or* and *Un chien andalou* and, with my brother, watched them every day for the weeklong duration of the mail order rental. MTV was a new treat too and we would stay up late for *120 Minutes*, the alternative music program where we got exposed to American bands—Stan Ridgway, Violent Femmes, The Descendents and Suicidal Tendencies became favorites—and kept up to date on the Brits—Peter Murphy, Big Audio Dynamite, Public Image Ltd and The Cure.

⋆ ⋆ ⋆

With salaried dollars flowing generously in, my parents started filling our pest-controlled house with things. One day, a computer was installed in the house. You had to talk code to it by lining up signs and letters over a black background, and use floppy disks for storage. A king-size waterbed throned in my parents' bedroom. In the backyard, there was the swimming pool where my brothers water-bombed and my hamster eventually drowned, and also the barbecue, acquired a few weeks after we moved in. The first evening she used it, my mother grilled huge steaks. The next evening, she did it again. And the evening after that. We had steaks at every dinner. I grew disgusted with red meat. The steaks were large, thick, heavy, and as inescapable on our plates as the air conditioning in our rooms. Ronald Reagan was on TV, proclaiming that America was back and its products the best. Buy American—but delocalize. It was 1985. The country yearned to put the Vietnam War behind once and for all. The ethos of the decade? Lean and mean was in. Trim the fat. Loosen the rules. Phoenix was a fast-spreading fungus growing under my fingernails. Keep competitive, edge to the top. Be afraid.

Things were going well by all appearances, both for my family and for the state of Arizona. So what if speculation magnate and mega crook Charles Keating was de facto in charge of urban planning? Weren't houses being built, one entire neighborhood at a time, and jobs plentiful? My brother and I used to sneak into the Keating construction sites at night, through loosely secured fences, to explore the empty shells of houses. Ghosts in ghostly rooms, we hid behind stacks of drywall when a car rolled by, scampering like coyotes from our artificial dens. Nothing could go wrong for America. It was great, they said and I started religiously watching the McNeil Lehrer News Hour to understand why. My father would read books on "zero defect" manufacturing for his job in an industry in direct competition with the Japanese—they knew a thing or two about leanness, and staying in line. In the West though, these concepts—"zero defect", no waste—seemed utterly foreign—expansion was a way of life, expeditiousness a remedy to self-doubt—but they could be adapted and people tamed into frictionless cogs, was the belief. "Zero defect" was rammed down the throats of factory workers and management alike, who all espoused that if business is good, America is good, and everyone is good. The job my father had been hired to do must have entailed swallowing hook, party line, and the company sinker. Did any of these principles rub off into our family dynamics? Teenagers were not very efficient. Could we be "zero defect" kids?

But we weren't and would never be. My brothers and I were growing up. Just like the adults around us, we now had the means to get things and we got them. Beers, poppers and smokes. We hung out at the mall with friends who spent part-time wages earned from McDonald's jobs on clothes and concert tickets. Gas was cheap, and putting on a keg party was a small investment. The right musical instruments and cars conferred prestige—sixteen-year-old boys picking up a guitar to pick up girls, teenage princesses pulling up in candy-red Camaros to a desert party. We tendered and bartered. We compared all we acquired. Overarchingly, independence was dangled in front of us kids like the most desirable outcome of growing up, but it felt like a tease.

It was of course a time of transition for my family. New country, new friends to be made, a language to master and a culture to absorb and digest. We closed ranks tightly in an effort to assimilate and I felt the breath of my parents' anxieties on my neck. It was bad timing. The last thing that I, a teenager, needed was to lose the little independence I had carved for myself in

France before our move to the air-conditioned bubble. I was reminded how I felt after skipping ahead one year to junior high school, when my parents, anxious to do well—and that I do well in a more challenging academic environment—had closed ranks around me. That gigantic fridge, these manicured streets? My mother's hysterical embracing of a barbecue, and my father's faith in a computer that promised to keep obsolescence—his own, inevitable—at bay? It all became too much. Could I make these things, these people irrelevant to me, foreign?

I could be free only in what I did to myself, to my own body.

★ ★ ★

But I wasn't yet fully in control and it filled me with silent rage, as on that mystifying time I was driven to the local supermarket by my mother to stand on a bathroom scale she pulled down from a shelf—we had no scale at home. I sneered, finding her unexplained request puzzling, and refusing to see it for what it was. The words she didn't pronounce were, I decided, in a strange, coded language I didn't care to speak. Translucent teen-me clocked in at ninety-nine pounds. We had a number for the situation but, like clueless heisters, we made out from the store empty-handed, after she replaced the scale back on its shelf. I had just been weighed on the cheap. What was my mother thinking? I felt cheapened. I wasn't even worth the investment of a twenty-dollar scale. Was she exculpating herself?

★ ★ ★

I remained an almost-round hundred pounds—I knew, even without a scale, because I was gleefully pulling my bracelets all the way up to my shoulder—through the summer. At the beginning of the new school year, my thinness attracted attention on campus. Teachers, secretaries, and students inquired about my health. It bothered me.

Something snapped.

I started eating again.

A lot.

Within a month, I shot up forty pounds. That's how bad I didn't want to attract attention. I was truly going into hiding this time. I would not be found out ever again.

I wanted to be left alone.

17

I'M RUNNING, RUNNING LATE for yoga class. I race, turn the corner at the tattoo shop, race down the alley—need to compose myself—and push the studio door.

Why am I running?

I had an arresting *séance* with my astrologer and it ran overtime.

Training is over and I graduated—I got the paper to prove it this morning in the mail, my last name misspelled—but I've not broken the daily habit of a yoga workout. In a few days I'll be living in Palermo, as planned, where I'll have to keep up my yoga practice outside of a class setting. Enjoy, I tell myself, while it lasts, this plateau of serenity, the convenience of a familiar studio. Ninety minutes of Vinyasa, a half-hour to get to class, another half-hour to get back home. It's a big chunk of the day that I don't have to think about. Yes, I'm afraid of losing this bit of structure to my life and find comfort in abusing food instead. Should I leave Paris? What next? I'm not quite admitting to feeling lost or scared—too proud for that—but I feel I could use a little guidance, someone to talk to. Someone neutral for a light banter.

An astrologer! That makes absolute, beautiful sense, I thought. Directions from the sky. Let the stars do the hard work of steering this sinking ship of mine.

It's such a Tucson move. There, in the Wild West of healthcare, good shrinks and sensible doctors who respond to small currency denominations are the rarest of mountain lions. There, I learned to trust the skies before my own lab results. The one MD I would consult—we all trusted him in my circle because he discreetly handled our VD outbreaks and tended wholeheartedly to our posse of broke-ass musicians and half-junkies, to fragile old barrio nanas, and to latchkey knuckleheads for an Andrew Jackson or two at most—had killed himself over a heartbreak, it was rumored.

Over the weekend, I search online for the most reputable Parisian peddler of planetary charts. I have a hundred and fifty euros saved up from selling fifteen of my CDs and DVDs online, a one-way ticket to Palermo, and a big, brand new bag of cat food. I can blow some of that money on a reading. I sniff out one intriguing profile, that of a man with celebrity clients, some of them famous singers. I choose to take it as a good sign that we two can relate, and confirm an appointment.

"Married? Let's see. No, of course not. Married to your work." Well, he got that right. From the look of his living room/consultation den, the same could be said of my astrologer's relationship status. The double-paned, cinemascope windows on his ground floor open onto a quiet, narrow one-way street and, across it, a vacant lot with plenty of sky. This is as open-aired as you can get from street level in the 11th Arrondissement. I can picture him in this room, curtains drawn in the evening, caroling cats on the sofa, conjecturing with a bottle of wine and one of the zillion books shelved on his walls.

"I see genius here, and there. See, these lines all converging around this area. Yes, genius." Me? Who would have thunk? That's a good start. I'm hooked. Mildly interested in my future since I already know it inside out—it consists of no more than more of the same futile attempts at change—I'm still ready to believe a good story about myself, even one of missed opportunities.

"Genius, yes, for the occult." Affirmative, he keeps going over the astral chart he's drawn up from my essentials. I take it all in, not sure I understand his scribbles. Loving the attention, I forget to turn on the recording app and safekeep his pithies in the pit of my phone. Addictive tendencies, courtesy of my furthest frozen planets. No kidding, buddy. Takes one to know one. Copy that. As for being genial, if I remember correctly, the conclusion is supported by four or five colored lines bundling up on the lower right corner of the chart. Or did he say occult tendencies and a genius for addiction?

* * *

Last summer, while recording my third and last Tucson album, I got a third tattoo. This time, though, I didn't want to ink a heartbreak. This wasn't any longer about the men I had loved and lost, not about pain and suffering, vanquished or not. This would be about me, a celebration of who I was. I needed the tattoos to remind me and give me indelible strength. After a quick online search for drawings of Leo and Taurus, my two astrological signs, I found a winged lion and a winged bull I liked and downloaded, printed, and scaled them for reproduction on my skin. Flamboyantly stubborn or stubbornly flamboyant, the two astrological beasts—steady, earthy Taurus my sun, with show-off Leo the rising sign—became two mercenary creatures at my service. The medieval-looking beasts took prominent residence on my deltoids. Originally from a thirteenth-century church painting, they had been sketched some years later on a piece of parchment by a visitor, a mysterious French wandering *maître d'oeuvre*, Villard de Honnecourt. Eight centuries later, they found their way from Villard's notepad—now housed in the Paris city archives—onto the web. In the original painting—a descent of the cross, a popular theme in the Middle Ages for church adornments—the winged animals were hovering right and left above the body of Christ. I didn't need the dead man on my skin, so I Photoshopped cross, man-savior, and his weeping entourage out of the picture and kept the spirit animals. Now, with my arms extended in yoga Tree, it is me that lion and bull protect. I had managed to replace the Catholic cross and the body of Christ with my own, and loved the symbol very much. Move over, Jesus—there's a new martyr in town.

* * *

Snapping into focus on my yoga mat, I try to put aside the astrologer's words for the duration of the class. Only dark thing the guy mentioned was a health issue, a problem, disease maybe, hospital in five years. When I looked panicked, he calmed me down. "It will be all right." Nothing much else. I breathe. Yes, it will be all right.

I really enjoy the flow of asanas today. I feel good, very good, feel as close as I've ever felt to understanding why I am compelled to practice yoga. Yoga simply feels good. I move and it feels good, and I feel at peace with my body.

After class, the professor pulls me aside—I've put my shoes back on already, about to dash so that, alone, I can mull over the words of the astrologer—to ask if I still plan on moving to wherever I'm moving to, and if I might not instead consider staying in Paris to teach at the studio.

That's a surprise! Me? Yes, one year, a commitment until next summer. I'm flattered that I am needed. Apologizing for the crappy early bird slots, the professor asks if I'd take on the 7:30am classes on both Mondays and Fridays and teach them in English. Not the best times in the week but, hey, it's a start and some place to build from. Would I do it? I can give him my answer in a day or two, he says.

I think about it for a second. "Yes, I'll do it." And with that answer, I take a first swing at my glass menagerie. Isn't it time I stay put instead of running? This is a chance to go deeper into my yoga practice. Haven't I found a safe harbor at his studio?

Corita/Cage: "Rule One: Find a place you trust, and then try trusting it for a while." Oh, Sister Corita, you are right. I had a home already and now I see it. I'm of the studio, I belong, and I feel relieved. It's beyond me to want something and beyond me to ask but I know I want it when I see it so yes, yes and yes, I'll do it.

Reality is also that I'm broke and, unlike in Palermo where I would have to pay rent, I have a free place to stay in Paris. Plus—I admit, I've not entirely evolved beyond feeling competitive—I'm flattered to be one of the few special students in our class to graduate straight into a teaching position. But above it all, I do want to keep learning. I've just begun.

Find a place you trust and try trusting it for a while.

18

I FLY BACK HOME through the streets of Montmartre, my bicycle a winged machine powered by the thrill of a new adventure. I'm happy. I'm going to be a teacher. How scary. I'm happy. Oh, just jump in. You've been a teacher before, and to wilder crowds. Showtime! Still, I'm not ready.

At our studio—yes, mine too now—summers are a quiet affair. Teachers and students bail on holidays. Our maestro himself disappears for a couple of months to run small workshops in the countryside. Starting in late June, classes come up for grabs daily, allowing us newbies to get started teaching with little pressure in a deserted studio. Summer holidays are no joke in France, not for the kind of well-off people who come to my classes. Two or three weeks in an exotic country with the kids, followed by a long stay in a Mediterranean village with relatives, with a pool and farm animals. At the studio that week, I overheard excited mentions of trips to Marrakech and Cuba, fjord cruises, and AirBnBs in Spain. A half-dozen subbing offers are already floating my way—granted, not the best slots: early weekdays Level 1, ninety minutes Level 2 on a Friday evening, low-attendance no matter the period of the year. Sunny days, however, bring a level of casualness to the scheduling, and requests come up at the very last minute with no pretense of nanny emergency or a simple cold. Teaching to a class of two in a sweltering room is no competition to joining a canal-side picnic with friends or taking the kids to the Belleville park. I wait, afraid to commit yet.

One night, I am nudged by a dream.

* * *

I'm standing in the professor's living room, alone, sun streaming in. It's not a big place, but it's not small either. I don't know what it's like inside—I've never been there in real life nor, that I'm aware of, have any of the other students—but in my dream, I picture the room stocked with tall bamboos inside *grès* stoneware pots, a seagrass carpet that stretches to the curtained windows. I've just entered but there's no one here who could have let me in. Doors, keys, access, trespassing? None of that comes into the picture. I'm standing on the raised stage-like area between entrance and living room. I wait. Suddenly, I fall backward, snap stiff as a plank. I will be hitting the floor, no doubt, hitting it hard, skull smashing. It will be painful. Just before my head hits the ground, the professor, suddenly appearing out of nowhere, catches my fall and bounces me back up. I'm safe and standing strong and upright again.

Anointed, I wake up serene from this funny dream, confident that I am ready to take over a class.

And that's just what happens. A cup of yerba mate in hand, I go to open my email box and there it is: copied to all studio teachers, newbies included, a last-minute request to substitute for our professor. Victory lap around the table, I sign up on the spot. Challenge accepted, without doubt and with not just a bit of trepidation.

This assignment, my first? One and a half-hour of rigorous poses, a favorite of the studio's most hardcore devotees, the professor's weekly Level 3 Wednesday evening class is one I've religiously attended myself over the years. It is the studio's crown jewel and its most advanced class. As many men as women take this class. The humidity level hits 101 percent within an hour of our backbending flips. I've felt good in that class, distracted from myself by the demanding series of balances and splits. Back six, seven years ago when I found out about the studio, it was this demanding class that convinced me the guy knew his yoga and maybe even something about peace of mind.

I thought I knew teaching. In Tucson, I had accumulated years of subbing experience in all sorts of public schools within the district, handling high schoolers, special ed kids, and toddlers alike. I took on algebra classes, driver's ed, sports, band, even French. The district administration only required from substitutes that they hold a bachelor degree, any, and could come up with a clean fingerprint record. That was it. I was thrown into my first assignment with barely a manual on classroom procedures and, with a degree in filmmaking, I was far from trained for the job. But how much preparation would I have needed to push play on a VHS machine, praying the film would hold the kids' attention for the hour?

★ ★ ★

Here we go. There's that moment I love, the very instant that jolts me as the strike of a cuckoo clock. No turning back, the show has begun. Close your eyes, thumbs on chest, I instruct, and from there, I lead—trusting all will flow smoothly till the end of this, my first class. Why wouldn't it? I'm ready. After a month of daily two-hour "master practice"—our mould as teachers—I've completely internalized the progression of poses, I'm intimate with their timing, and I can pass as an authority on a trademarked sequence refined over many years. I am sitting cross-legged, my mat perpendicular to two rows of six mats that fill up the floor space. So much for scarce summer attendance. The class is full, the day gloriously warm. Sunlight teases in to brighten the recessed room, so much smaller than our ample training studio. After three Oms, their eyes open now, my twelve students slowly stretch the chest forward above lotus legs. Downward Dog next, please. I stand up and pace the narrow space between the rows of mats. From my own to the pillar to the back wall and back. This is my territory now. By the third Downward Dog, I stand with proprietary relish surveying two rows of behinds sticking up in the air. My class.

At the end, although I'm eager for feedback, I refrain from sheepishly asking my students how I did. Thankfully, the studio manager had warned me, "Don't let them know you're new at this." So true. I have to look up to a teacher. Students have to believe. That's the whole trick in making them feel like they've gotten a good deal for their time and money. I agree with the manager's advice. Fake it 'til you make it. It's the whole trick for me too at this point.

After the last student has gone, I shut the fogged ventilation window above the gargling water heater, stash away a forgotten shirt in the smelly dressing room, and shut off the light in the minuscule toilets. I pull from a small filing box the cardboard note cards that contain each student's account details, tallying up attendance for the second time—I don't want to make mistakes. It would be another year before the studio got equipped with a computer, and I can't wait. I, who spends most of my sentient hours on a Mac, am irked by the slow finger search for cards that rarely stick to their alphabetical lot in the box. I give up, frustrated that my eyes and my fingers are finding it difficult to coordinate with my brain in locating the right Marie.

* * *

Daily throughout the rest of the summer, I teach and take classes. Yoga is that magical candle that never stops burning and good little moth-me keeps circling it. I'm on a roll, a routine, buoyed by the prestige of the job. With the respite from self-harm granted by my devotion to physical practice, on a continual high from daily doses of exercise, I enjoy a temporary bout of happiness. Healthy even if by force of habit and inertia,

I hold my breath, relieved and rested to be puking twice a week instead of every single night.

At the studio, familiar faces, old and new, are becoming still more familiar. I warmly greet the girls who trained with me, whose names I finally bother to learn. But now that the dust has settled on new hires, we're de facto split in two groups. In one, the half-dozen who got invited to teach and in the other, those who didn't. Some, envious of my new position, make it known with pointed questions on what exactly I said to get the job, if I was approached or if I asked, and what *le prof* told me, and when.

I hope they are envious. This, being picked out of the lot, must mean something to someone. To me, it feels like an easy win in a game I wasn't playing. I didn't ask to teach here. I was not even going to stay in Paris but, now, I am back in the spotlight. Girls whisper in my ear and ask how I got what I have. I could very well shrink when probed by their stares but this time, I realize, I shouldn't. I won't. I know what I'm doing and have earned the right to be where I am and will not be kicking the bucket like a raging child who's not ready to play dress-up. I'm not bashful. This is my wedding party and I'm going to play the part of the smiling bride.

I know the drill. Downward Dog followed by Up Dog.... The first couple of weeks, I write it up on sheets of paper, little sketches of sticks for legs and bubbles for heads and torsos. It's not a perfect system, but it helps me move away from the sequences I learned and start making up my own, adding a stretch here, a vinyasa there. There's never a good place for my cheat sheets, though. I don't want them to be visible to my students. I know well from my performing experience that you can't hide anything from an audience, or so very little. Every move, every prop means something on a stage. Now in a yoga studio, my cheat sheets are saying I don't know what I'm doing, and I pull them out blushing.

A blur at first, these many chests and bones, my students. In beginners' classes, their panicked eyes give me chills as they erratically dart around the room. I can't answer their pleas. I am not their regular teacher, and they have to trust me, but I find it hard to comfort them with the personal attention they require. In advanced classes, I dread losing pace and being called out for the inexperienced teacher I am. I'm still as scared of them as they must be wary of me. If I sense one of my students taking the lead from me by transitioning to a pose before I call it, I lose confidence in my teaching and get angry at the dissident. Yet, although I'm just the sub, I do really want to give them my best. But I still can't look at the shoulders, ribs, and bellies of my students. I'm afraid to read too much into these limbs, afraid to care and feel their presence. I remain aloof and safe.

Day by day, though, faces come into focus as I grow more confident in my teaching. I begin to notice mouths that I want to wipe free of tension and eyebrows free of twitches. I even begin to care and cringe at every bowed and pinched back in need of some TLC. Oh, people. Learning to read the room, I plunge ahead with my set of skills and hum through the summer, dipping my joystick into the honeypot of body default modes and their corresponding mental zaniness. Bodies are fascinating. I didn't think it would matter so much to me but I do want to help my students. For now, I can only go stand in front of them, on my side of the barrier, and do what I'm expected to, nothing more and nothing less. I'm still a parrot.

This could be fun.

19

"THAT'S QUITE A LIFE."

Well, yes. Thanks. It is quite a life.

"You seem to be doing just fine."

I suppose.

But wait, how would he know? He's just a kid, white-bloused maybe, but a kid, a hospital intern wielding a notepad and a busy pen in an attempt to look the part of a seasoned clinical specialist. He's flanked by a young woman, his skinny sidekick who, while we're having this conversation, stares me down from the top of her quarter-century. In truth, I believe, she is not paying attention, contemplating instead, I imagine, matters of greater importance than my affliction—things like swiping and huffing addictions. How would they know if I'm telling convenient truths?

I'm doing fine. I won't debate it with him—maybe he's

right. Of course, he is. In theory, my visit to this specialized hospital unit makes great sense. After the lucky break of getting a teaching job I didn't ask for but now see as a chance to get my life in order, I'm giving myself one year to stay put—a sabbatical from running away. And I would get help. The hospital visit is a first step—astrologer aside—toward seeking it from the right places. I'm in a great country for that, one that can boast of a decent healthcare safety net, and in a city with a plethora of mental health professionals.

Only a couple minutes into the interview, though, the two kids have already lost my trust when I realize that I know more about my bad habits than they do. Why else would they be excitedly asking where online they can watch my music videos? Don't they realize I'm only too eager to share—and hide behind—my accomplishments to avoid answering questions about my health? I balk, feeling like I've beaten them at a game I've played for longer than they've both been on this earth. Yes, I'm doing fine, I say, wholeheartedly agreeing with them. That's exactly my problem. "I'm doing fine," is all I know to say.

20

"I HAVE AN IDEA."

Doctor fingers around his cool, white smartphone, looking for a number.

"Let me call this friend of mine. He's a busy one, but he might be willing to help you."

I get iPhone envy for a second—see myself swashbuckling it away from his hands—but regain my equanimity by looking through the window to the swaying swag of chestnut trees. I'm anxious for a distraction.

Since the last hospital visit fiasco, I haven't given up. The pointless interview by the two white-bloused kids confirmed only that I knew how to find and knock on the doors of reputable establishments—in other words, work the system. Methodically, I studied my options and knocked on another door for help, this one in leafy 8th Arrondissement, a few streets away from Place de l'Étoile.

As the doctor rings up his friend, I tense up. Why change? Absolutely nothing wrong with my current beater of a phone. Why, even if the clunker has been freezing up lately at the least opportune times, why on earth would I spend money to trade up the ol' phone?

Why change? Indeed, I could keep going, managing my idiosyncratic behavior as best I can, admittedly freezing up once in a while but still somehow plowing through life.

My life? Four years in, my Blackberry phone and I have had a pretty good run. Just look at all these concerts' backstage passes stickered on the frayed case. And inside? Photos of saguaro cactuses? I took them. Airport screens listing departures to New York, Istanbul, London, Munich, Paris, Brussels? I stood below, excited, hopeful. Crisp crickets on sticks at a food stall in Beijing, lava stone walls of an earthquake-shaken, roofless church in Lyttelton, New Zealand, snaps of Cat napping on a red-striped serape, and a bizarre red chile plant reclining in its pot in the green room of my favorite music venue in Austria. These are all memories I treasure. Oh, hang on to the old beater phone, hang on to it 'til it croaks.

Is there really anything about myself I want to change at this point? Like this phone, I hold within a collection of rainbows, skid marks and sunset shots, some hazier than others. Can I change? If I'm to believe my astrologer, I can stop fretting right now. I can change neither past—the man nailed it when he sketched the unique diagram of my first five decades with bright crayons over my birth chart—nor future—assuming I'll live that long, the main events of the next two or three decades are also highlighted on the printout.

"Woman, in her mid-forties. Been bulimic since her

twenties. Can I send her to you?"

True fact. If you put it like the doctor puts it to his colleague on the phone, my case does sound pretty straightforward. Stripped naked of particulars, I am this; a woman in her mid-forties, long stuck skipping like a record needle over a two-note melody. Although I only hear my doctor's side of the conversation, this is the first time I hear myself, and my "peculiarities," being discussed freely in front of me. I don't know if I like it. He used the b-word, bulimia. I don't ever speak that word myself. Save for that one time during my anorexia when I overheard a young cousin, unbound as she was by our own family's unspoken rules of silence concerning my health, comment to my brother on how skinny I looked, I have not heard my case aired out in public. Hush, hush. Don't ask, don't tell. That was the motto in my family back then and I was only too happy to oblige.

Oh, I am freezing now. Damn A/C. I hate it. The cold air in the room has blasted all thoughts out of my head. I don't know what I feel anymore or what I am doing here. Like a child throwing a tantrum, a silent one in my case, I am lashing back at whatever is in range, ranting at the first thing—A/C—on which to fixate. Cold suddenly, tired, disheartened. I don't want to change. Should I leave?

"Yes, I understand. Of course. Yes, yes, I'll see you there. Thanks."

Doctor slowly places his phone back on the desk.

I ask, "What did he say?"

"He said... very difficult."

Doctor tells me, in a soothing, "I'm your buddy" voice, that his friend is not optimistic about my chances for recovery. Tells me his friend believes it's very hard to change at so late a stage in the disease. Doctor looks for words. Doctor stops short of saying it's impossible, but I hear it loud and clear across the desk.

Okay.

Damn A/C.

I'm all shook up now.

Impossible? There goes the French anthem. *Impossible, c'est impossible*. We'll see. Maybe it is. And then maybe, just maybe, my pride is pricked.

What is it I learned in yoga? Stick with the pose. Don't go running. There's nowhere to hide when it's you versus yourself. I'm starting to feel like the lessons learned in daily practice are sinking in on a deeper level. Breathe, stay in the pose. All will pass.

I won't give up. I ask him if I can call his friend myself about scheduling an appointment.

Doctor gives me the number.

Back in the street, I'm still shaking. This was a big, courageous step, discussing myself openly, as frankly as possible, with someone who listened. Opening up. Oh, I know what's going to happen later when I get home. I can taste the bile already. Had to be done. Had to see this doctor. But at what price? Hang in there. Don't. Don't go running to the boulangerie.

It most certainly is *impossible*. But words have been spoken, out in the clear. Impossible maybe, but possible starts with the smallest step.

The hospital interview was a cop-out, I realize. I didn't want to be cured. I wanted to check all the boxes, ace the test like a good student. But I've put one foot in front of the other, one tiny step and I'm intrigued. How is it I get better? How does that machine work?

That afternoon from home, I call and leave a message for the doctor's friend. Call again a few days later. Leave a second message.

Despite the choice introduction by his colleague, Mr. It's Impossible never calls back.

That pisses me off.

21

NOW, IT IS A *very good girl. And how well she's learned her lessons.* Cat on my lap, sounding like a granny fawning over a favorite brat, I mock myself and my achievements but it is the truth. I have learned my lessons. Mornings to most nights, I practice, read the assigned books and teach, teach and practice, and read. With not much time for anything else, time flies in the halfway house, and I am surprised when I get to bed that I haven't thought of binging that day.

All that has been mine—feelings of accomplishment in the recording studio, joys and excitement on stage but also the dread of keeping up with new music releases, marketing trends, up-and-coming labels and hotshot booking agencies—all that is on hold through the summer. I slow down. Until further notice, no shows—oh, just that one coming up in Paris in the fall, the one I wouldn't turn down despite Cat's warning— and no music pressing to be recorded, released, or promoted. No photo shoots, no videos—always so worrisome, how I look. Life made very simple, thanks to no rent and no bills. Just me and Cat, who I must remember to feed and remember to talk to, yes, of course, to talk to and love.

In the quiet of the apartment on those short-shadowed summer afternoons, I stand on the balcony for a few precious minutes of contemplation, melting into the muted light streaming through the leaves. The low distant humming of city traffic resembles the bumbling of bees and lawnmowers that I associate with summer in the countryside. Flies bumble around and large insects crawl into the room. Cat scratches and yawns. I stretch on the mat, and Cat sneaks on there too. She likes to be close, curls up on my belly when I read, jumps on the bed every morning at seven and wakes me. Save for taciturn bugs, we haven't been visited by anyone. A sparrow knocks itself out on the glass of a tall window, but I get to it before Cat does. Evenings, I curl up on the couch, the warming, glowing screen at my side statically purveying redacted humans. Nothing wrong can happen to us. Cat's no Henri Gloom, the Gallic feline YouTube sensation. Her daily habits—from a favorite way to lay on the blanket to the ten times ten licks she gives herself every afternoon after snacking—my now-regular grooming, the regularity of my hours of rise and sleep, sameness of foods ingested and digested daily, the very evenness of my consumption of space and time, all keep me stable. One night, Cat catches a flirty little mouse in the kitchen. It's what she does. The air is drier now. Water tastes chlorinated, chalky all right. It's summer. I know the lay of these rooms by heart and Cat and I call it home, here, now. My suitcases are stashed in the closet. Their Tucson smell has faded.

* * *

In August, I manage to go fourteen days without puking—a victory that I don't ostentatiously celebrate, out of superstitious fear. Fingers crossed that nasty habit is on the way out. There are plenty of other little habits, however, that stick: like stepping out of bed every morning and stepping straight onto the bathroom scale, popping a Levothyrox pill, making tea, feeding Cat. I don't mind those. Who would I be without them? I hold my breath. Two weeks. What if this is the beginning of… what if I am…?

Baby steps. Slow down and sleep eighteen hours a day if that's what's in your nature. Pieces of myself are sliding back into place. I try all sorts of good and normal grooming things—the kind that were luxuries these past few years of hotel life on tour, like brushing my teeth regularly and thoroughly for five whole minutes three times a day, or separating the trash in green, brown, and everything-else bins. At home, I drink tea from the same favorite cup every day and eat with my favorite fork. Licking her fur, Cat approves. Fleetingly, I get what safe could feel like—slow heartbeat, anxiety lifted, deep breathing, and steady, a smile.

Evenings now, after a warm day, I look out from our fourth floor through the crown of the chestnut tree and its roosting pigeons. With my neighbors' windows also open, all sorts of intimate sounds bounce about the courtyard, bits of voices and music from ground level to the *chambres de bonnes*. The sounds mash up into a lively communal coo. The first month here, I kept the windows shut at all times. I didn't want to hear or see anyone and was afraid to be heard and seen myself. One evening, in a *Rear Window* moment, classical opera from the second floor rams Pharrell's *Happy* looping from the fifth, and a crying baby rhapsodies through the nightly newscast. I smile. I stare at Cat. Cat stares back. Are we okay? We are okay. Thank you. No, thank you, says the fur that swipes my bare legs.

★ ★ ★

September rolls around. After a summer of subbing, I now have my own classes. This schedule will carry me through next summer and my one year commitment to the studio. I'm ready.

My first day, September 5th, a Monday, no one shows up to my 7:00am class.

Again, no one at my second class that Friday, also at 7:00am.

The following week, one student on Monday but zero on Friday.

No matter the dismal body count, I still bounce from bed on Mondays and Fridays to get to the studio on time, eager to give my all to my students. By the end of September, attendance has stabilized at two. My devotees are both French, a distribution I wasn't anticipating as the professor had asked me to teach my two classes in English. I translated the words of French that made up the sequence I had trained for, used as many Sanskrit names of poses as I could remember and came up with a bilingual class that would work, I believed, for both French and English speakers. I want the Americans, though. I know the yoga they like and I'm fluent in it. Where would I find my tribe? I make up a purple and white logo from the photo of a bendy woman in Eagle pose, write up a short description of my offerings and post the news on the bulletin boards of expat groups, the American Church in Paris, and competing yoga studios. On a mission to raise the attendance, I get a thousand small fliers printed but end up tossing them away after realizing I lack the conviction to go door-to-door in the 11th Arrondissement. I'm going to have to work my numbers up in a different way. No other teacher goes to such lengths to promote themselves, and the studio manager isn't expecting it. I'm used to self-promotion—I do it for my music—but this is different. This is a chance to learn to do things differently. Trust my work. They will come, and come back. In Paris, do as the Parisians, I keep muttering to myself, hoping it will stop me from spinning my competitive wheels needlessly. Plenty to do anyhow.

I have to get to the studio early. There's a bucket list of things to check out before the first student walks in. I switch on the lights and assess the damage from the previous day. Dust and hair, tissues on the ground, disheveled mats, and stuffed wastebaskets. I vacuum the whole space, replace old towels in the bathroom, refill toilet paper, wipe the sink, prepare class props, line up pens, aerate the room, place the clock near so I can see it during class and wait. From the get-go, I consciously try to do those tasks thoroughly, as I would a moving meditation. I practice not cutting corners.

There's no direct sunlight into the studio at any point during the day. It is located at ground level in the courtyard of a tall, early twentieth-century apartment building. The room, ten by ten meters in size, is encumbered by two large, awkward pillars holding the ceiling, and the lack of direct light keeps it cool and dark like water in a deep well. I imagine I am the sunbeam and bring in life.

It's a hell of an early time to practice anywhere, 7:00am, but especially in this country. I get the early-rising nationals—a few late-season American tourists and a couple of Germans—but, as it turns out, one of my first somewhat-regular students is French, a lawyer. The woman—in her early thirties and flowy in that stiff *Grandes Ecoles* way—is well practiced and disciplined. When I first see her, I get an immediate sense her hips and lower spine are beginning to stiffen up, freezing her movements ever so slightly. I shake my head. Am I starting to imagine things about people and their bodies? How could I read her in a split second and decide she could use some hip-opening poses?

One morning, the woman tells me how happy she is to have found this class. She loves that it is early and taught in English, and that she can double-up on two of her resolutions, the first being to exercise and the second to work on her language skills. All this self-improvement and she can still be at the office by 9:30am. She's a labor and employment lawyer. I picture her on a dance floor, shuffling assuredly at a debutante ball on her way to a successful career. Oh, she says, she also absolutely loves my classes because, often my only student, she gets individual lessons for the fifteen euros a group class costs.

Hasn't she just told me she worked in labor law? I flinch and think it ironic that she doesn't seem to realize how much I am getting paid to take care of her, and her exclusively. I ponder if I shouldn't hire her to look into the regularity of getting paid 3.25 euros for her ninety-minute, one-on-one class—our rate is per student. The following month, she stops coming soon after attendance increases by a handful more people when I can't lavish any longer my undivided attention on her alone. A fine example of the bargain hunter she was, a cutthroat hoarder of the *bon plan*. She disappears from my life and I am left feeling like I have been Grouponed.

22

GOLD CONFETTI, THEY SHIMMER so, above my lifted, reaching hands, twirling in slow motion around my bare shoulders, and, relenting, come down, down to rest, there, on the ragged stage floor. Ah, the impermanence of my golden flies.

I throw another fistful into the air.

A blinding spotlight aimed at the stage, from beyond, into my face and I can't see—won't see—past the twinkling lint suspended in the sweep of light. Not one to cry over spent flint, I shift my attention to the gold sparkles on my forearms, show-glitter glued on my skin before I walk on stage to stand and sing. Up, up, keep on, with a child's ravishment at all that flickers. Keep up the happy. Yes, show them the way. Show them, all who have come here to watch, show them with your warmth, with your voice, that this heart is a magical place.

★ ★ ★

September had rolled into town, summer-struck and sunburned, and hung tight for some weeks when suddenly, one chilly morning, it was autumn in Montmartre and, at last, the much desired and dreaded night of my show at the Louxor theater. At home, Cat has been coughing, often. I am worried. It's painful to watch her retch her little lungs out. She crouches, her tiny body heaves and shrinks with each rasping cough. Is she sick? The fits are getting more frequent. Just this week, her daily sprints through the apartment—usually at about 10:00am—have been interrupted by her gasping for air. Is it asthma, lung disease or, as the veterinarian implies when I bring her in, an abnormal heart condition? Big, enlarged heart? Oh, Cat, big-hearted Cat! That's my luck. Fine. I schedule Cat for an X-ray with a specialist.

I've been pretty good in the weeks leading up to this. Pacing myself, with only half a dozen puking fits in as many weeks, I've managed to stay healthier this month than through the whole year. Such a deadline helps. It is something I so look forward to. If I don't pinch myself, I'll think of myself as always having been that calm, meditating yoga teacher living mostly on the wagon in Paris. Pfff. Bring back the wild, golden child. Give me a stage. I miss myself.

It is a big party in this palace of cinema, a venerable old building, between Deco and Nouveau, renovated with public funds back to its 1920s glory. What a grande dame of a building, rising four floors above the Magenta Boulevard, next door to the cheap wedding suits and a stone's throw from the Montmartre hill. Push past carts of corn on the cob peddlers. Enter, leaving behind on the sidewalk bearded men pushing baby strollers of groceries and black marketeers Marlboro packs. Behind the ticket counter, the staircase to top-floor heaven, the little café with a terrace overlooking the busy intersection of Barbès with Rochechouart. Faux marble on the walls and flapper-era winks of exoticism on its vaulted themed ceilings, Louxor is a face-lifted beauty. We will perform under the muted gaze of four gold-winged plaster scarabs ensconced on top of their papyrus columns, and I'm nervous.

Granted, I haven't played since I left the States six months ago, and this is an unusual arrangement, a private concert in a location untested for a live performance. It is a worrisome setup, one I don't control. Why am I worried? I'm here at the invitation of an old friend who is celebrating the twentieth anniversary of her very successful company. I briefly worked alongside her then, a hunter chasing down the first American indie films she would distribute in France. I loved the treasure trail and even considered for a time staying on in Paris to work with her. But that was not to be. However much I was compelled, in comfortable second-tiered position, to help out—for free, for fun, for the beauty of the work—I just wasn't cut out for the 9-to-5. My friend's verdict back then? I was unmanageable. Taking that as a compliment, I hightailed it back across the Atlantic, more broke than I'd been in a long while, moving to Tucson where I was to remain, living cheaply all these years. I had burned-out in Los Angeles and been burned in Paris. In Tucson, I kept doing pretty much whatever I wanted with my time, wasting it included. No, I couldn't be managed by anyone but myself. Arduous road, scary prospect, but ultimately, it was my delicious fate.

And see, I came back on my own terms, a singer now. Yes, the old friend who found me unfit for her offices now wants me to sing at her party. Yes, of course, she'd pay for my bandmate to fly over from the States, but no, I wouldn't get any money. Well, I didn't care about the fee. She had me. I wanted in for the sake of playing one more show with my American bandmate since I liked very much the music we made together.

And then, bells and bullhorn, the show. I take off my uniform, the jogging pants and yoga shirt, loose, easy, shapeless now, comfortable. Comb the hair and burnish the skin. My bandmate flies in from Seattle. We rehearse for a few hours in a studio just beyond the *périphérique*, the ring road that surrounds the city and divides the old from the new Paris. The big night comes, and I wonder what it will take for me to learn to say no. Learn to not want, not desire, nor grasp. I'm the sort to seek out and believe bad reviews more than good ones. They always seem so much more instructive. But tonight, yet again, I am this someone else, dressed in gold lamé, and I take what's mine, feeling like a thief and a fraud once again.

I go stand on stage under the plaster scarabs. The room hushes, and the first guitar notes ring out. I bow to the audience and turn halfway around, ceremoniously lifting a hand toward the movie screen on the back wall to point at the twenty-foot-tall lizard beamed from a photo file I gave earlier to the house projectionist. Except, I'm looking at a blank screen. The lizard isn't there. Oh, damn. Someone's asleep at the wheel. Should I say something? The audience won't know anything is missing, right? They were not expecting a slide show. Maybe it's better this way. How do you explain a lizard? Here it is! I see the light change on stage, a new glow from behind. The lizard appears, on its back, front legs rigidly extending upward. It has no tail, no back legs. Cat sliced those off, eating or discarding the bottom half. I need the photo to cryptically address the ambivalence I feel about my own belly, and that I am half the woman I would be if I wasn't bulimic. Not that I want to make it clear. I only need the reptile as a hint that my songs will not be all saccharine. This much will be understood tonight. I sigh in relief and make a mental note to thank the projectionist by name—oh, what is his name, and that of the sound guy?—at the end of the show.

Nothing matters at this moment beyond my microphone, the curves of his guitar, and my radiant bandmate. This is our little world and there is nothing, nothing behind the walls of this great, big hall. I'm a child, I'm a woman, I'm anything I care to be, and all who watch and egg on the fantasy are accomplices of mine. Ready for this one? Let me give it to you, our covenant, with all my heartfelt love and compassion, my song *Mouton Bercail*. Here we go. *J'en ai fait des hôtels et des caves*. Yes, hotels and cellars, goes the line. I've puked in them, and so many other rented, borrowed, and begged-for places. *J'en ai perdu du temps*. Yes, I've lost time. So much time. *J'en ai bavé, du sang*. Drooled blood. *J'en ai fait des erreurs*. I've made mistakes. *Je suis faite comme ça*. This is how I am. *Je ne changerai pas*. I will not change. *Et j'en ferai encore. Encore. Encore*. I will fuck up again. Again. And again.

* * *

The concert ends. I'm drained. I find myself at the upstairs bar, surrounded with people in festive moods. My bandmate, intent on remaining dry and getting some rest, has already left the theater. Tomorrow, he will fly to Berlin to play in front of twenty thousand people.

How could tonight not have gone wrong? I haven't played with him in months. He's on a massive world tour backing a pop star—to his credit, he did not want to cancel our Paris show. How could his head be here with me? I wish he had stayed. I too should leave the party. I know that if I stay, I'll regret it. I'm afraid. But I linger, hoping for a kind word. Maybe from my press agent, if he made it, as promised, to the show.

This is not my party. I hear nothing from anyone, as I heard nothing from my father the first time I played in front of him. Which of the two, my father or I, was more terrified that night, I don't know. It was a long time ago already, five years maybe. It wasn't a good show. That night, I made all the rookie mistakes. I warmed up my voice outside in the back alley—in February. I wore very few clothes onstage in the drafty venue—a converted train station. And, in the first row, I could not help but see my parents looking at me. Three songs into the set, my voice was a rasp, gone from stress and cold. I turned to my guitar player and gestured, swiftly sliding my hand across my throat. I was done. After I stepped off, embarrassed but relieved my ordeal was over, I went straight to my parents. My mother stumbled a few words. That was atypical. She has a way of drowning herself and others in speech whenever she feels uncomfortable. My father didn't say a word. That was typical of him. He never said much.

That wasn't always a bad thing.

To this day, I can't recall a single instance when I was given words of encouragement or praise from my father for my smarts, my looks, or my achievements but, when, barely nineteen, I took off by myself for Nicaragua, just in time to reach Managua on the tenth anniversary of the Sandinista revolution, my father didn't say anything to prevent me from going. It still baffles me to this day. The tiny country was at war with the United States, I didn't speak a word of Spanish, and I didn't know anyone there but I had my parents' support for the trip.

My father never came back to another concert of mine. Maybe he felt he was not in his element—and he wasn't. At least, I have to give it to him, he knew to make himself scarce. Who was I—this person, his daughter, on a stage with high heels and a top barely covering her skinny chest, winking and swaying and cooing demurely? I was simply hard at work—too hard maybe—patching my torn identity on stage, straddling two models of femininity, the innocent and the feline, and seducing my audience. Certainly, my father wasn't in the way, but he wasn't very much there either.

What would he have thought of my Louxor show? Nights like tonight, it's just a whole big mess, an unfocused and self-defeating performance, oddly both grandiloquent and disengaged. I find my press agent at the bar. He is blunt, as always. "Where is the essence of your songs? Get back to the essence," he shrugs, poking right where it hurts. Essence? Isn't that where all signs have been pointing in both my yoga and meditation training? And now, this unlikely—unlikely?—source: my agent?

The next morning, I wave goodbye to my friend in the taxi that's taking him to catch a flight to Berlin. He was already asleep when I got back last night and we rushed out of the door this morning, a fast farewell. Tonight, he'll play for more people than I'll ever play to in all my life. I can't even imagine what it's like, the electricity of those twenty thousand pairs of eyes. We haven't discussed our own show. What is there to say? I'm sad to see him go, more heartbroken than I let on, and all my strength, bundled these past weeks in anticipation of the show, flows down the gutter at the taxi stand. This is it. Alone. I can't yet admit it to myself as we hug goodbye, but I don't see how we can keep doing shows together.

With him gone, I turn around on my heels, hurrying back home before… milk and bread, bread and milk, bread. No. I can resist. Hurry. But there is a boulangerie on the way and… in just a few minutes, I won't feel sadness, I won't feel anything any longer.

An hour later, the breadcrumbs are strewn like confetti on the kitchen floor. Over. Onward. When will this stop? After I tidy up the mess, I make another cleanup effort, this time on my own thoughts. To nudge myself to think about something else, something positive. What if I took care of what I needed to take care of now, today, this minute. Here. As in yoga, come back to the breath. Be here, present. I keep saying it in my classes. Why not do it myself? This would be new and helpful. Fall seven times, pick yourself up eight. Take a deep breath. Don't think. Just breathe.

After ten minutes of meditation, I open my eyes. I know. I'm going on a sabbatical from the stage. I won't attempt to book shows. I won't accept any. I owe it to myself to remove temporarily that source of confusion and stress, so I can work, work hard at ending the bulimia. I'm so certain this is the right decision that I pick up Cat from the couch for a joyful spin around the room. I'm resetting the counter. From today, no performing for a year. Seriously.

★ ★ ★

The X-rays have confirmed it. Cat has a normal heart. Her fits of coughing aren't due to the organ cramping her lungs. I have nothing to worry about. But why is she coughing? The veterinarian doesn't know nor does he seem too worried. Could be a host of things; she could be allergic to something. Is this veterinarian giving up on us? I will have to resolve this by myself.

Home, I look for patterns in her fits. Does she hate being here so much? Is it psychosomatic? Oh, I'm losing it. Cat's only a cat, why worry? After a few days of detective guesswork, during which I pay attention to when she coughs and how she stops, I understand.

My Cat. Oh, yes, she is allergic all right. I'm reading the news one morning when it all clicks. Pollution! This whole week has been one of the worst of the year for particle levels. The coughing exactly coincides with those peaks of pollution. On days I feel tired and can't stand keeping my contact lenses in for more than a few hours, on those days when cars and trucks should rest at standstill to let humans, trees, and animals breathe, on those days, Cat coughs.

How simple was that? Cat, along with every single animal, plant, bug, and human in this city, is breathing foul air. And yes, Cat and I do live in the worst Paris district for pollution, close to the *périphérique*, along densely stacked thoroughfares to the center of town. Ah, poor thing. And me, how does the air affect me? I'm not coughing. These particles, this water too, chemically altered? Ain't no place to raise Cat. I'm pissed.

Who's in charge of this dump? Ain't no place to live, but I can't go away quite yet. I just started on my sabbatical, and I still have someone to see. Someone who can really help.

23

I GO BACK TO my shrink.

"Back" isn't the right word. I never stopped going. It's just been fifteen years since my last therapy session.

The year was 1997. Newlywed, I had been living in Paris for a few months already. I would remain there until I finished editing my second, hour-long documentary film, and delivered it to the French network that financed its production.

A couple of things weren't going too bad for me that year. Although I wasn't comfortable bragging about my new status to anyone—I liked to explain it had been a pure administrative formality for the sake of immigrating my boyfriend to the States—I couldn't help but feel, a married woman now, more secure. My film—it featured members of a lowrider bicycles club I belonged to, and dealt with issues of cultural appropriation between the Anglo and Chicano communities of Tucson—needed me too. I owed it to the members to finish the editing and bring it back to Arizona for a screening. I was as close to happy as I could be, with close companionship and lots of sex with a man who was never stingy about telling me I was beautiful. Despite still puking, with the energy and optimism of the young, and a hefty dose of denial of the long-term consequences of my sickness, I was not overly distressed by the continuing assaults on my body. Loved, I felt worthy enough of a change, and was able to turn my attention to my own health. Things were as peachy as they would be that decade.

★ ★ ★

My psychiatrist's office was in the 15th Arrondissement, one block away from the Swiss Village, an odd compound of unexciting specialty shops that felt so out of place in this pallid urban mush of tall residential buildings that I became very fond of it. I wandered through its courtyard every week, guessing it to be the least appreciated of the minor tourist attractions in Paris. The sessions did me good for a few months until I abruptly decided to return to the States, putting a sudden end to the progress we had made toward some slow but real results. Yes, I was fleeing, as my *psy* noted. No, he didn't believe in phone consultations. I wasn't serious about getting better. But things weren't that bad, were they?

Fifteen years later, nothing much has changed at the Swiss Village. The shops are still there and the people who populate them still few. My doc's doorbell also sounds equal to itself. Under it, his name is unchanged, set on the same copper plate.

The door, however, doesn't open as well as it used to, and I have to slam it shut. In the waiting room there is now a radio set and, on the walls, two one-blink-worthy reproduction prints: the first a rather melancholic woman with a tilted head, and the second a pastoral scene of an eerily serene couple of lovers.

Doc is a psychiatrist on the loose from the eating disorders services of the famed Hôtel-Dieu public hospital. Someone there had recommended I call him, with a voice that sounded caring and pragmatic. I trusted the recommendation and scheduled a first visit. Fifteen years ago, his practice was teamed up with that of a nutritionist, a plump woman who smiled a lot, weighed me, and gave me, the food snob, recommendations on what to eat and how. She suggested I stock up on those zero fat, fake sugar, low calorie but filling yogurts which, even at the time, made me cringe for their lack of actual nutritional value. I knew better, didn't I? Despite my distrust of aspartame, it was a relief to be allowed sweet indulgences by a higher authority. As instructed, I gobbled up the yogurts, colorful and fluffy as Casimir, the kind TV monster from my childhood. The nutritionist was working from the base of people who still felt green beans as integral to a meal as a glass of water, but I was coming from the land of yesterday's pizza for breakfast and blueberry pop tarts for dinner. Fifteen years ago, I felt ahead of the curve in France when it came to the evils of pre-packaged and artificial food. Today, the world knows better, mostly.

The door opens. My turn. Of course, I'm nervous. This guy is going to look at me straight for an hour without saying much, and I can't sing-and-dance to get out of it. This isn't a show, categorically not a show, and Doc is just about the worst audience anyone can have, as dead-fish unresponsive as audiences from...—no, I won't name names.

Like his office, the man doesn't look like he has changed much. I probably haven't changed either. He has a large, firm but supple handshake and a steady stare. The armchair that was by his desk, almost touching it, is now in the middle of the room, a lot further away from him.

An hour later, I walk out remembering the little but significant victories we wrought out from our few sessions fifteen years ago. There was that time when I held my head back up in what felt like a pivotal move. I had managed to extricate myself from my catatonic stance, and looped thoughts to get back on track with our conversation, carrying my half of it to engage the relationship at hand. That brief, important moment, which was duly noted and immediately voiced back to me by Doc, was my most assertive grasping of reality, a small tilt up of head, eyes and thoughts away from a dark and lonely stupor. It was that bad, back then, once all my smoke mirrors were cleared. Instantly, Doc had wisely mirrored that victory back to me, and I felt prouder, stronger, truer, and a bit more alive at that instant than I had been feeling in a long time. I never forgot that small gesture, looking up.

Fast forward to 2013 and my expectations have become more precise, my time shorter maybe. Now, I need support from someone who will listen to me talk about writing a book. After more than twenty-five years of this sickness, my life and addiction have become so completely intertwined that, in truth, I don't even ask, don't really hope to be cured. I just don't want to let it be a waste. I have decided I will write about my tribulations. For that I can ask his help. I have put myself in charge.

24

SOME DAYS LATER....

Damn it. Hurry the fuck up. My turn now to order.

In line now, I stand rustling inside a boulangerie I've never been in before, waiting to order the whole freaking pastry shelf.

Yes, again, I'm in a boulangerie—where else? But I've never before been in this particularly fine establishment on the Left Bank. It will do. It's conveniently on the way to the train station.

I'm picking up a friend there in an hour. He's from Tucson, an All-American hometown boy, not shy of a towering six feet three and behold, bald-headed of what would be blond strands. He'll be staying overnight in Paris on his way back to the States. I left Tucson six months ago. It'll be good to see someone from home and catch up on the gossip.

Got an hour to kill still.

I am tired, yes, I admit. Maybe just tired of the crowds. It doesn't take much to make what I call a crowd. Just avoiding one person on the sidewalk, that little dance that's necessary to not brush that person's elbow or to avoid a look, to not be noticed and not pay any attention, not entering someone's space—well that's enough to make a sidewalk crowded. I wish I were in bed sleeping it off.

I thought earlier that I might go see a movie in a Quartier Latin art house. It wasn't meant to be. Only a couple minutes ago, stomach growling, breathing shallower, I stood waiting for the green man at the intersection of boulevard Saint-Germain and rue de Buci, licking fingers clean of greasy juice and hankering for more spicy fat to suck. Chest tightened, teeth clenched and the jaw protrudes forward like the buzz-cut chin of some Lightyear ragdoll. Here we go again.

The pungency of the lamb lingers on my fingers, the invisible ink to the lines of instructions for what follows next. I already feel it in my mouth. Next is chocolate, and it slinks down the throat.

Would I have enough time to go home, go all the way across Paris and take care of this… this indulgence and be back in time at the station? I can puke it all in less time than it would take you to slip your shoes off and pour yourself a highball. So do I, can I, can I keep stuffing my face, go home, empty out and be at the station in time? Yes, technically, it's possible. I've fathomed crazier crosstown management trips before. I'm wearing my white knee-high boots. Style under duress, I walk tough. I could do it.

An hour to go, a few minutes.

It is October. A couple of weeks after the Louxor concert. The seventeenth of the month, most definitely. I won't forget that date for a while.

On rue de Rennes, a flux of cars. And blinking lights, loud buses, and pretty bicycles, a magma of sounds that jingle and ring, faces that ricochet on faces, eyes that wander, shoulders and men in shiny costumes, and shoes I glimpse, in mirrors everywhere, every shop display a no and every boulangerie a yes, a resounding yes. If there is a soundtrack for isolation and loneliness, it is this and it is loud and blinks, blinks like a Christmas strand. In that cage, I have my hands in my face, stuffing myself with self-love and self-loathing in equal amounts and....

And then I stop.

Ess teh o and pae, I s-t-o-p, stop.

Yes. I mean, "this" stops. I don't stop the moving, the walking, I don't stop the eating, but in my head or wherever these things get decided, I've stopped. Not stopped not-breathing, not-living and not stopped stuffing my face. No. I've stopped the fretting. I will not puke anymore.

Yes, I had enough. *Basta, bastante, assez*. I give up.

I don't stop, no, not this day nor the next, not for the next weeks and months, I don't stop walking into boulangerie after boulangerie. Oh cities! Nor do I stop buying the next bag of brownies ten times over. Matter of fact, that October day, I keep doing that until and after I get to the train station.

But I stop fretting. I give me up. I will not puke anymore. Let it start there, my salvation. I stop thinking stuffing needs puking. From now on, I'll stop before I vomit, throw overboard, retch, stuff the toilet, flood the pipes, clear the toxins, scrub the guts, smell the death star, lick the toad. I'm keeping the chocolates for myself.

Something clicks. Something has clicked.

Fuck it, you did it.

Now deal with it.

Eat.

Go on with your day.

Standing still, yes, on the sidewalk on rue de Rennes in the lowly light of a late afternoon at the early onset of winter, I'm embracing the weird and twisted. I can't go on like that. So what if you've eaten a mountain? Just deal with it. Grow up. Be it, or as a friend once said to me—about my music but she could have said it of my life—"shit or get off the pot."

★ ★ ★

I make it to the train station in a state of quasi-meltdown. The towering clock belts out six over the glass entrance hall. More even than safety-ruled airports, stations—not trains necessarily—run on time. Stations are time. They allow as much interaction, playful for me, with time as I've found anywhere. Plan to get there, to catch a scheduled train. Map your steps and, with a little luck and some strategizing, make it just on time, and win like a child who places a bet on the sun setting. Play the elbowing race, toy with the gentle stress of making it on time.

Below the clock, glass doors sliding at intervals erupt a flash of black-clad commuters. My friend's train arrives in twelve minutes now, on platform twelve. Ah, chicken fumes are radiating out of the pores of my nasal wings—always the first spot on my body whose sweaty emissions I can smell, the crest glands in such close proximity to sensory neurons, giving out signals of whatever it is I have ingested in the preceding minutes. And chicken—something in its chemical composition—is the worst offender, the fastest transmitter. You there, say the nostrils, you can't fool me. I can tell. You had flabby, pumped-up, nonorganic, industrial chicken breasts for lunch. Oh, yes, you're absolutely right. How did you guess?

I'm going mad. Nostrils lightly twitching, I move into the warmth of the station womb. While I've got you on the line, weren't those orchids I smelled in your stools this morning? But yes, certainly, they were. How did you know? Never mind. Can I ask a favor? Could you scratch us gently and maybe possibly move a few steps to the left, please? Why? You're pitting against our sun. What? Yes, against this clock tower. So move just a little. I comply, stepping away from the faded yellow of the setting sun.

I'm losing it. What kind of a twisted, hypnotic playground is this?

At the departure level, I'm waiting in line at a take-out food joint to order a sandwich. Something about ordering chicken sandwiches inside a train station makes me feel patriotic, like I'm fulfilling my duty in service to an American notion of patriotic unity. Keep consuming, they said after the towers fell. But really what these stern upholders of the nation's integrity were saying was to put on our blinders. Left alone then to make sense of our diminished reality, we coped the best we could and obeyed. Cellophane-wrapped, manufactured half-baguettes, expensive certainly if you consider the price of depressed tomatoes, radioactive-white feta crumbs, and fibrous and rubbery filets of meats. Ah, this is fun. I'm insanely excited, a new feeling, an odd mixture of power and helplessness, a release. Great. I still have ten minutes to finish this sandwich and eat another. Any freaking sandwich I want.

Years back, I had this notion that it might be healthy to go through an apple juice cleanse. I drank gallons of the stuff—and neither drank nor ate anything else—for five days straight in yet another ill-fated experiment. By the second day, I could taste cigarettes in my mouth without actually smoking, and soon felt like every single poison I had ever ingested before the granny detox had come back to haunt me. I can't remember why I felt I should subject myself to this radical diet. Maybe at the time it was in fashion among my friends. Alcohol, sex, sugar, credit cards, we were all trying to kick one thing or the other. By the third day of the experiment, grinding my teeth from the acid of the juice and mad with sugar ups-and-downs, I knew what metals really tasted like. Blood in my mouth after I puke always brings to my mind the empty gallon glass bottles lined up on my Tucson back porch.

It's October and colder, dark soon like a too-early evening. I don't care. It is what it is. I feel warm, from the food and the walk, October be damned. I made me warm.

Yes, what if, at last, what if I just kept it all in? Would the ground split open and the black plague return? What if I just did what I wanted, ate what I wanted, bought, sold, did the deed now and here, here and now, and just dealt with it? Would anyone get hurt? Would I? Stop fighting.

Up I go on an escalator. I relax a bit, the short time of the ride, my two feet now securely set on one step. A numbness overpowers me, a truce as I stand still in movement. Lifted up as if by a magic trick, invoking Tati and his modern machines, I am on a great joy ride in a massive amusement park. Distracted at last from myself, I look around like a wide-eyed child on her first trip to the dream factory. What an immense train station hall, what grand walls. So cathedral-airy and tall that pigeons and sparrows wage battles overhead.

I've been so clean and kept so pure despite, or thanks to, the puking. What if I dealt with having a body? With the sensations that come from overeating, from slushing junk food, ingesting sugar and fats, croissants after éclairs, éclairs after quiches, quiches and everybody's favorite foods and sinful treats? A sabbatical from salads in bile dressings. How about it, stepping on the road less traveled for an hour or even a couple of minutes, just to feel what it's like? All it would take is one brief moment, a split second of recognition, to know I am not a slave to myself, to taste freedom. What if there were new sensations to feel? And what about pleasure?

Real warmth, all the way to my toes. Ah, yes, calories from food, the fiery byproducts from the furnace of my metabolism. It's started, the breaking down of matter, the alchemical transformation of want into will. I plant my heels in the ashes of many past resolves and stubbornly refuse to budge from my vanquishing position. I am not going to puke. I am not puking! I am in hot-as-hell hell. Not quite pleasure yet, ah. And the body digests while the mind wanders, and the two have never been so far apart. And yet, it's got to hit rock bottom first.

Now squirming on the train platform, I wait. Three minutes to go and one last sandwich to polish off. I can't escape. Bodies in clothes walking toward and then past me. I'm disappearing myself. Not gazing into anyone's eyes, not staring at anyone, perfecting the art of transparence. I think of what it would look like to actually be busy. I seem like I have something to do, that I have all the right in the world to be standing there, waiting—but do I? What a relief to have a purpose and stand there for a good reason. What a joke too.

Here he is, my hometown buddy. We hug on the platform. "Hi. How are you? How was your trip?"

It blows my mind that I can actually utter those words, any words. How was your trip? Really? I'm amazed that I can listen to the answer, nod in agreement, then think of another question, maybe even suggest something for us to do. That I exist still, despite having repeatedly stabbed myself into oblivion with a hundred cookies and five or twenty tarts, three thousand sandwiches, and then some more in the past hour.

I guide us through the station and into the metro, the numb leading the bald. He's so much taller than me, a gentle giant in the underground tunnel, towering above the flow of train riders. We make an odd team. I smile through the pain that has started taking hold of my stomach, my distended, bloated, so very full stomach. We make our way home. I show him his room. He drops the suitcase. I suggest dinner. Dinner? I bought a ticket to that sky coaster ride and I'm not getting off. I shall be normal. How about kebabs, I suggest.

Yes, I'll have dinner too. The man must be hungry, and I take care of hungry men. The man looks like he is not afraid of food. And tonight, I'm not either. I'll just be normal and normal is to want dinner in the evening, right? So we head down the boulevard because evening meals are what we do, because people break bread with family, friends and strangers, because we are humans. God, I love pain.

I suggest some cheap alternatives, the kind of places that this man would be eating at if he was home—and I would too, in love with a taco truck on the side of the road in South Tucson.

The first kebab joint does not appeal, with sickly neon light, flaccid meats and an uninspiring cook. At this point, I couldn't care less; should but I don't. I'm gonna enjoy whatever it is we'll be having, and which I never, ever treat myself to. A meal—shared, warm, social. So we keep moving up rue Ordener.

The second kebab place we find is smaller. Lebanese probably, with tables close-knit on the floor, and with couples or solo souls, people with identities and functions partaking of a meal together in relative anonymity. The white-haired and mustached cook behind the counter seems to care about providing some sort of haven to his nightly brood, and seems genuinely happy making kebabs, stuffing breads, aerating the tabouli, each sauce a tender ointment over his meats. I order a liver sandwich, just about the oddest, grossest thing I could find on the menu, something I would never order in regular times. Liver marinated in herbs, strong to the taste, repugnant if I think of it too long. I let it linger in my mouth.

I'm disgusted. I'm disgusting. I eat the whole thing. Showing barely a flicker of the discomfort I feel, I'm an Oscar-worthy actress in a really slow food-porn movie. Is it through yoga practice or meditating that I have perfected this frozen, impermeable look on my face? Is that the look of least discomfort I put on for those around me? Whatever it is, it's mighty useful. I can still function and I can still be of use to my American friend who doesn't know his way around this city. Shut up and get out of your head. You might be useful to someone. It might not be so bad.

"So, how are things back home?" I ask, and without waiting for an answer, inquire about his tour through Europe, and his week of surfing on the Basque coast. He looks up from his kebab, struggling to find an answer. I don't let him, burying his attempt with yet another question, about his plans for a future album. I don't remember his answers, if any, to the canned questions I'm spewing out, some of which I had already asked on the way from the station. I wish I could take a breath, be, just be at this table in silence with a friend, both of us eating quietly, unhurriedly, and trusting.

We walk back home. I am moving like a barrel, my belly pushing up against my jeans, my shirt, my jacket, bombasted. Oh, I give up. I want to scream. I'm in pain. He asks about the yoga classes I teach. My speech is slowing down, words slurring, comatose from food. Say it. Just say it. Scream it! See this? This is me. Hurting myself. Scream it.

Oh, my classes? I shrug.

It's tough, I tell him and stop at that. Pause, turn my tongue seven times inside my mouth, speak only the truth and only if truly required. Is that how it works? Somehow, despite the impeded flow of my straight and narrow thoughts, I am still able to communicate what needs to be said, nothing more, nothing less—classes going well but it's tough—and do what needs to be done.

★ ★ ★

So there. A friend came to town and we hugged in a station. In truth, I don't think much of it—or him—in the moment, obsessed as I am by that, my first glorious day of saying no and no more. Desperately needing to believe I've won that battle at last, I don't see that the real victory hinges on a much more discreet event that evening. I know it now. Tonight after dinner, I was able to utter one little word of my truth to a friend, not a hired hand, not a stranger. This is my butterfly moment in the greater war. Maybe because he's more transient than myself even, gone by morning, I can confess to this unthreatening friend that I'm struggling with my teaching. Because I've exhausted myself with a massive food intake and my defenses are temporarily down as a result, I blurt out true feelings of fear and self-doubt. Teaching is hard work, I admit. I don't know if I'll ever be any good at it. I'm scared to find out, I say. Being honest? That wasn't so hard, was it? Walk in. Beam and get the job done. No more, no less. Maybe later, I can even crack a joke.

25

I AM WIPED OUT and slip into bed exhausted and raw. When I fall asleep at last, moaning, after an hour of the ol' toss and turn, I can only manage short, dreamless bouts of relief from the furnace within. I wake up, again and again, achy, flustered by gutty rumblings, and kick the covers, then the sheets. Too strung out to read, too shamefully derelict to get a kick from a YouTube dose of *Daily Show* antics, I'm terrified of getting up, afraid that if I try making chamomile tea or take a shower, I'll run into my friend—or wake him—and have to be sociable, and hospitable, and put on an act. That seems like so much effort, and for what? But maybe I'm most afraid that he'll glimpse my ugly side, the short-tempered, dismissive and flighty child I could very well snap into if I get up. Funny how having someone around can make you feel even lonelier and more exhausted.

So I lay frozen in bed, sweating but unable to chill, and I try to find solace in the thought that this is truly and finally the beginning of a new era. Ah, yes, I can speak, tweet, and post all day long, every day, about my work—a well-shorn carapace of commitments—but here in this bed, I only wish I could simply, unremarkably just have a dream. I haven't dreamed in months, just like, for the whole of last year while on tour, I didn't have a period. Just like I haven't had sex in months. All systems down. I might not have taken more than a couple breaths that whole year either. Oh, yes, things can and will only get better from here. I convince myself of it, spinning the prospect in my head like so many fluffy sheep until I fall asleep on my back, belly bursting up to the ceiling, the only laying position that's not painful tonight.

★ ★ ★

The alarm squeaks. I squash it. It's 6:00am. I was sleeping. Dark out, dreadful in. Nevertheless, I have to soldier on to class. Got a job to do and a routine to uphold. I am a yoga teacher now. My word, I gave my *prof*—yes, I'll do it. It's the one commitment holding me together at this stage. I must keep it together, no matter if this is the first day of the rest of my sans-puke life and I've got the glucose hangover of the century.

So I get up, go to the toilet and pee noisily, glad that my friend isn't around to hear that funny, intimate sound. He left before I woke to catch a flight back to the States, rounding out weeks of touring in Europe with his tripped-out 1970s psych solo class act. Did he tell me last night how glad he was that he'd soon drop his bags in his own home soon, sleep at last in his own bed and, not least, get some real tacos? Lucky him. It wasn't like that for me. I had started touring right around the time I split up with my husband of twelve years, running away from our nasty breakup. After a couple years on the road, I hadn't bothered making much of a home, except for Cat, who held down the fort as best she could. If it hadn't been for her, I would have kept running after my tours ended. Musicians who, after being away for months, gracefully re-enter their lives amaze me. I envy them the ability to slip back into familiar home routines. Some have a mate who provides that stability—and keeps the plants watered during their absence. Others are good at disconnecting or can delegate, with managers, bandleaders, or family members handling the ceaseless behind-the-scenes work of music. No matter. Over two, then three, four, five years of touring, I don't think I was ever able to gently land "home." Junkie-me missed the adrenaline of the stage, the nightly high. My spectacular crash landings ultimately led to the depressing realization that I didn't have much of a home anymore and didn't feel like making one either.

I don't know how my friend felt when he left Paris this morning. I don't know because he didn't tell me. When did I give him a chance to speak, and would I have even heard him? His stayover was a missed opportunity. Ships in the night, we passed. Now I'm glad for the darkness, to be alone again.

I go to the bathroom. Cat peeks in but doesn't get my attention. No love. I feel the same way I always do when rising to catch an early plane before a string of shows. Tense, apprehensive, grumbling from a short anxious night and the dreadful logistics of packing but in automatic pilot mode. Like every single morning, I pull out the scale and step on it, as mindless a step as brushing of the teeth and splashing of rose water. I hold my breath like I've been doing every morning since the day I bought my first scale.

Fifty-seven kilos. A hundred twenty-five and a half pounds. I've gained five pounds since leaving Tucson. Nothing to be worried about, likely just yoga muscle, not fat, picked up during training and, since then, my weight has remained stable. I'm not completely comfortable with my current weight—when have I ever been? Deep down, this oh-so-fat singing lady is still mourning her anorexic frame, the perfect number reached once in a lifetime, the round hundred pounds. I was seventeen years old then, with permanent bruises on my ankles where the bones, protruding without padding, routinely knocked against car doors or the blunt legs of chairs and tables. When walking, my ankles also pounced against one another, turning black and blue. Back then my skinny limbs were like the small silver milagros brought to an altar for good luck and a miracle. My arms were tiny, my belly was shrunk and my butt had flattened. Hands, heads, lungs, pricks, and ovaries as amulets to mend a broken heart, ward off diseases and spells, cure infertility or deafness, and bring prosperity. I could have cut myself up in pieces and, little coin-sized charms soaked in wishes and imbued with prayers, disposed of the parts at my favorite Tucson shrine, El Tiradito.

In the kitchen, there is a thank-you note from my friend. I'm glad to see it. I pop a Levothyrox pill and boil water to make yerba mate tea. I force myself to wipe out some pancakes, thinking that I should not be afraid, in my new puke-less life, of keeping up good habits of balanced meals and healthy breakfasts. Important, isn't it, to have and hold breakfast no matter how full still from the evening feast. I make enough pancakes for two people, and polish them off standing by the range. A healthy breakfast maybe, in ingredients at least, but certainly a consolation prize comforting me for having to leave bed.

Those salad days were short-lived, six months of delirious purity from self-abnegation, resolute like some mystic dieter, the perfect anorexic. In waking dreams, witches would appear to me, a delirium brought on by lack of food, in an atrophy of the body that exalted my senses but depleted the ability to derive any pleasure from them. My body was sacred, virginal, magical, and holy, but my mind was a cellar of pagan rites. I was visited by wise old sorcerers and sat in ritual circles with angelic beings. These images were enthralling. I felt like I was allowed a glimpse at a private, coded passage from childhood into womanhood, and would be led to experience that transition on my own terms, to be understood subterraneously. The reality on the surface wasn't as exciting.

Quite the contrary. Leaving my too obviously anorexic self behind at seventeen, I padded myself to the brink with cookies and cream. Puffing back almost overnight from my all-time record low of a near-hundred pounds, I crept up twenty pounds at the start of the new school year in an effort to avoid scrutiny. The anorexic me was an object of desire, as I had seen over the summer when a French man twice my age had picked me up on the street, brought me to his apartment. After we listened to some records and kissed, the man said he wanted to know me—which I misunderstood, of course, in the biblical sense. Virgin-me got scared by my own curiosity and cluelessness, and I ran for shelter. If my beautiful body was indeed a lightning rod for sex, adulthood, womanhood, and death, all related in my mind, then I would make myself ugly and fat, and disappear. I languished at a nondescript weight until I was about twenty-two, yo-yoing between a hundred and twenty and a hundred and thirty pounds until I discovered that I could put two fingers down my throat to slim down.

I was living in Los Angeles then, at the height of the aerobic sport trend of the '80s. Beautiful California. Obsessed with good looks. I got my first boyfriend—a nice, southern white boy and budding filmmaker like me—and lived with him for three years despite not loving him very much, staying because we were making a film together and I was raised to stand by my man—or behind him as was more likely. While in that loveless but pragmatic relationship, I discovered—my aha! moment—how easy it was to make myself puke. The new practice, and my not shaving my legs for months—a horrific sight to the dear boy—did us in. The film was nearing completion, we didn't need each other's help for it any longer, and we split up. As I had seen my mother do during her entire married life, I had stood by, staying put well beyond what my self-esteem should have allowed. But this is how I learned to be a woman, brought up, as I saw it, by a good, dutiful daughter from a hard-working farming family, self-sacrificing mother and supportive wife to an ambitious, capable, and emotionally-stunted man.

After I myself got married—ambitious, capable, and stunted like my father; as self-denying and conflicted as my mother—I shot up to a hundred and forty pounds. To this day, I'm still not sure why I got bigger after marriage. I suppose I felt stuck, felt like a cat awkwardly treading over a puddle. Shifting shape from single and depressed to married and having to hide my depression was neither natural nor enjoyable. To a newborn, pounds gained or lost weigh in the balance between life and death. Maybe I never got over that simple equation and liked to believe I was a specter child, unwanted and unloved, parentless.

★ ★ ★

Cat meows. Her bowl is empty. I feel guilty leaving her alone again. Ah, I should bring her to class. Wouldn't that be hilarious? Cat on a mat. Cat hopping over styrofoam props and tossing about eye pillows. If I did bring her, I wouldn't be feeling like such a cold, uncaring bitch, leaving her home to chase her own tail for hours on end. Tidying up the kitchen counter, perfunctorily cleaning the dishes, I glance again at my friend's note. I'm glad we didn't cross paths this morning. The note—from a lucky someone, to be headed back as he is now to sunny Tucson—makes me lose my resolve. Seeing my friend off with a hug? I would have closed the door behind him and teared up. What for? Blue sky mornings and the restless desert winds? I feel conflicted for the first time since I left. What if I went back? Wouldn't it be easier? It is home, or it was, for such a long time. Couldn't I be fine there now? Unlike here, the sun would be out already at this early morning hour. I miss the light. What am I doing? Cat needs the outdoors. Wasn't that selfish to bring her here, in these dreadfully walled-in rooms, while I sorted out my own shit?

Outside is clammy, October making a pass at December. Light hasn't broken out yet, the sidewalk clear but for frumpy dog walkers as I turn the corner toward the bike station. Two minutes into the ride, I'm in a sweat. The incline of rue Ramey is steep this morning. I'm not feeling particularly good. Unspent still, last night's food intake fuels this morning's fire. Puffing, I make it to the top of rue Christiani and turn left toward boulevard Barbès. I pedal slowly, huffing along even on this slight downgrade. I slide along Magenta, skid by slippery-wet République, left to Voltaire and lock the bike at Richard-Lenoir, my cotton shirt now fully drenched under the hooded sweater. Oh, I am hoping no one will be at the studio waiting for me. Please, let no one show up for class. I want so badly to get back home, to hit the computer and distract myself online with the uneasy stream of fluctuating burps, massive churning, and felicitous farts of the world-wired expresarios of my tribe. Or just head to bed and wake in the spring.

The studio's courtyard is dark still as I enter, and very quiet. On the floors above, a couple of kitchens are bleakly lit. It's a matter of minutes before the commuters' ballet begins, with feet stomping down the staircases and sidestepping puddles in the courtyard, with the street door slamming shut behind each little worker bee pulsing out into the flow of pedestrians, buses, and kites. Standing at the studio door, I search through my bag for the key, fish it out, and open. I step in and take my shoes off, place them on the rack to the left. I turn the lights on and walk to the teacher's desk. I drop my bag down, turn the computer on, letting it wake grudgingly as I go to the dressing room. In the bathroom, I switch towels—dirty for clean, empty out the trash can, refill toilet paper. From behind a curtain, I pull out the vacuum cleaner. By now, it is 7:29 or 7:30 depending on where I look. I wish I could stop time right then, in the in-between place where all is spotless and I am in the right, doing right for once. Just doing my job, nothing more and nothing less.

I replace the vacuum cleaner in its resting place and I go to the fretting computer to open a new registration session. Anyone? I'm here now. Why not come? Ah, a gentle knock, a soft pushing of the door. Timidly, the first student walks in. Damn, damn. I can't escape now. What if this is the only student to come? Would I have the guts to say, hey, listen, I can't do class for just one person. You go home. Go away. No, I wouldn't do that. I wouldn't say something like that because it's not much different from when I sing to an audience of one. I always pick up something in the process, and curiosity—or a vital need to learn—ultimately will always get this cat.

So I teach class for one student. And if I had felt shell-shocked from the minute I woke up, by the time I start class, giving it my full attention as easily as if I'd done it all my life, I am forgetting these past twelve aching hours and I relax in the stress of a new, urgent, and involving task. With only one student, my guinea pig, I find myself giving lots of hands-on corrections, not shying away from close contact and physical touch. The practice fast gets more intimate than a regular class would allow as I look into the unique case, with permission implicitly granted, of this person and her body. It's as if my student had laid out a map to her own self on the mat and I was reading it like a storybook, leafing through the lifetime of choices that shaped this body into its present self.

Inching her left foot further forward to strengthen a Triangle pose, pointing at a sleepy muscle to spruce it up, taking shoulders and pulling them back and down… my gestures are gentle, the indications subtle but I am getting the responses I need. My student is working as hard as I am. What more could I ask of her? We're a team. I find the wordless things to say—whatever works, however loudly or softly it needs to be spoken—so that this body in my care wakes from slumber and lazy habits, wakes and stirs so that life moves in, and change is allowed. Feel yourself reaching up. I stop myself from talking further. Less is more. Suggest. I become the breath that paces the movements. Be like me, visit your body's most-forgotten rooms with the curiosity of a child, the casualness and readiness of a cat. My fingertip tapping her on the back, I ask for the breath to make home there, inviting movement in trickle and spurt, inviting joy.

The hour of class passes quickly. That surprises me. I didn't think about myself much at all, little time to feel sorry for my bellyaches. For an hour, I looked beyond myself toward another body, another being, in a selfless gesture of compassionate caring. I don't realize then, that first morning, how much of a relief that is, how much I needed that, and how happy it's making me. Digestion has begun!

26

SOMEHOW, SLOWLY, AGONIZINGLY, OVER the course of the next couple of months, I keep up my resolve to not puke ever, ever again. What a miracle these two months are. Nine weeks, two days and sixteen hours precisely, the longest stretch in over ten years that I've capoted over toilet bowls solely for the purpose of sitting legs spread and pondering the wonders of biological life while waiting, the digestion process having been allowed to take place at its own time and pace, for food to be expelled from my body in the god-granted and soundly biological downward way. Yes, it has to start somewhere and I've struck a deal with myself—no more puking—not a perfect deal but it will do for the time being. It must.

* * *

I may not be puking for now, and that's great, but things aren't exactly peachy during those sixty-five days. Supersizing myself, I balloon up a scary sixteen pounds and get the urge to take daily notes, recording each pound and ache, my hopes and fears cursived in staple-bound notebooks. A day rarely amounts to much of interest under the dark orange cover, later ones in fire red and pitch black. Some days, I write just a line or two, but each time the words on the page smack me dumb with their syllabic arrogance, their letters altered by anxiety into brisk demons. They gleefully rub against each other, twisted, undecipherable in places. Pain. Headache. Extra fries. Discomfort. Eyeless rat. Page after page, on and over and around the blue lines, death-masked syllables caracole. Heat. Thirst. Pig. Aching. Sugar. In layers and rings of shape-shifted lines, truncated words cavort in rutting cascades. Soaking. High. Sleep. Stir. Dumpster. Letter by spastic letter, word by sniveling word, I take note. Pull the tablecloth. Finish your plate. Lick it clean. Caffeine squint. Hell. Hate. It doesn't feel like a victory yet but I'm at least facing my own monstrous tale without the eraser pen.

Dutiful, unrelenting in my commitment to the experiment, I blow up by a pound or two each week, like a white goose stuffed with the infinity hand crank from heaven. I forget, really forget what hunger feels like. Super-duper bottomless cups of fat are now my weapon of choice in proving a point I'd rather not be making for my own sake. Or would I? Am I not enjoying this guiltless abandon, this absence of worries? This new lightness? I can eat whatever I want, anytime I want, and I do not fret. Yes, time for myself and whatever I want to do with myself, in exchange for dresses that won't zip up.

No more rules. No "12-hour window." No "you shall not mix meats and starch." Adios to "sugar is as addictive as coke: avoid both but especially sugar." I finish my plates. Mind control, all of it, directives from outside and above that I burn at the stakes of my newfound rootedness. I am free to eat anything, no longer the obsessive quinoa queen. That "wheat is the root of my problem and so is milk, butter, cheese—but not goat cheese" religion? Gone. Cheesecakes, my new allegiance. Bring them on. I let go of all my rules, all at once. Gluten? Dah. Go for it. Rice? Absolutely, but with everything else on top, and what's wrong with white, not brown, rice? Meats? Yeah, why not? I can't fathom a vegetarian diet right now. I'll have to reassess at a later time whether I should be eating things that once walked or swam or flew. Tortilla chips, no salsa? Hell yeah. Sounds lots better than salsa *sans* chips. Save me first, the world will have to wait. No vegetables for a week? I don't miss them. A shot of whiskey as I walk in the door? Give it a try. It's worked for so many. A beer? Whoa. Cheers.

Supersizing-me indeed and just like that hilarious and sad movie, day in, day out for weeks, I eat plenty of whatever the hell I want to eat, whenever I feel like eating it. And just like its poor, mad, reckless, self-experimenting director, I get the headaches and the bellyaches and the gas and the joint aches and the depression. I am perpetually numb and, no matter the outside temperature, warm as if wrapped in a wool blanket inside a fur coat next to a coal furnace. My belly rounds as if I had just swallowed a cow and her calf. My skin changes texture and I look like a manatee, thick and waxy. Patches of reddish blotches poke out on my face. I fart black birds. Giraffe skin, I also grow fangs and fins, retooled, yes, as the creature I truly am. With bursting glands, I'm sweating all the time and, no, not in flashes. I live under a constant sun. My underarms smell like the bottom of a swamp, my skin flaps like chicken. I wonder if Cat knows that. I counteract the inopportune odors with generous sprays of Untitled, my go-to perfume. But our beautiful chemistry is altered now, the idyll is over. The very green perfume—part bitter citric juice—hisses when I splash it on my changed skin. I switch to sweeter, more gentle Féerie—a scent I couldn't stand until now for its cloying violets—and, behold, we match.

Alas, who am I becoming if my favorite perfume doesn't recognize me anymore? Am I turning into a sugarplum? I have gas, I am bloated, and I stink? Well, may just be I am alive after all. A body. I'm definitely not a cat. Cat wouldn't put herself through these nine stations of hell.

My mother didn't buy perfumes. She didn't wear makeup. Her shoes were as flat as her breasts were discreet. Except for those few, odd months when she primped up at beauty salons, she seemed content *au naturel*. Lipstick, French tips, eyebrow waxing? She didn't model for me how to grow up into and enjoy—master—makeup and satin *négligés*, and my own body. I had to find my own way. I liked stories, and perfumes were stories, my own intersecting those told by marketers. Long before my Untitled and the fantastically regressive Féerie, before even Angel, gifted by my then-husband in what might have been a wishful bout of self-serving generosity, I had another favorite: the opulent Opium, an odd choice for the shy, starving teenager who would not dare fully fashion herself as a femme fatale but was happy to dream. The heavy scent kept me clothed and warm through my teenage years and gave a sheen to the monotone suburbs of Phoenix. I dropped Opium right after anorexia, at the same time that I stopped smoking. I didn't have much heart any longer for little rebellions such as cigarettes and fatale scents. When I started eating again, I became transparent at last.

Except for the smell.

★ ★ ★

Stinking? Long before the puking stench, there was plain and simple sweat stink bomb, and being called on it by my new classmates in the Phoenix high school, the teenage nightmare *par excellence* that no amount of exotic perfume can make go away. Eating as I was then, loads and loads, I smelled something strong, something else. I bothered. Somebody ratted. I got called in to the principal's office. A student in one of my classes—may have been someone in driver's ed, the class just after lunch when I would sweat the most walking outdoors through campus—had complained. Maybe there were complaints from all of the classes, from the entire student body, each and every person in that school—someone denounced me, someone who was threatened that I didn't smell of Teen Spirit. The school principal was decent in an Old Spice sort of way and, seemingly understanding, pinned it all on another culture's habit of not showering as much as was needed and certainly not as much as was customary in the United States. "Different ways," he said. I was a latchkey kid to my own empty house, body divorced from awareness and both working odd hours. “This here is Arizona,” he said. “It’s hot, very hot.” I sweat, you sweat, we all sweat. Yes, no kidding, it’s hot, hell hot, and we all sweat but the kids here, they take five showers a day each day. In a desert we patch with swimming pools, the kids of plenty take showers before and after they dip their toes in their parents’ backyard ponds. Us kids, high school age demiurges of the strongest nation on earth during the Reagan era, we were the cleanest—most sanitized—people on the surface of the earth. More intolerable than an eyesore, the one who stinks, the untranslatable nose-irritant, is the true alien to the surface-clean people of this insane suburban block of Arizona.

Not that I wasn’t showering at least once a day. But that wasn’t enough. I would have ingested much, so much food for breakfast, provisioning with bags of cookies and cereals and milk and toasts, that by the time I left the house, my sweat glands were on high alert. Mother only once remarked on my morning habits, saying they were expensive. Her reaction was as incomprehensible to me as her driving me to the supermarket to weigh myself. Could she have been lacking in grace that badly? Did she only know to leave me in the care of a veterinarian like a debilitated cow on her parents’ farm? By the time lunch rolled around four hours later, I would be sweating profusely indoors, no matter how much conditioned air our classes were injected with. It was 112 degrees outside, 69 inside the school and the McDonald’s restaurant three blocks from the campus. Without skipping a beat, we would sweater-up on cue, prepared always with extra layers. Me, I was out of step with this populace, and yet we were many: a silent army of female ghosts, thinning and growing hair on our arms and overlip, shaking with cold, fear and glory, and later, having resumed ingestion, stinking and farting, burping and blowing. So it was bound to happen. I got called to the office where I was admonished and told to buy some soap. That was the low point of my high school year. I was Pepé Le Pewed. I'd been found out, outed as the glandular French stink bomb, clearly and unequivocally decreed repulsive.

I waited out the end of hot days, one cookie and one cookie jar at a time, climbing inexorably back up the scale from my sickly double digits weight. Some weeks later, around Halloween, when temperatures at last fell short of the triple digits mark, I'd already regained twenty pounds and was left alone, unremarkable, undetected for the rest of the year. No, I don't miss high school.

27

COME ON, ZIP UP! Hold your breath.

It won't, I can't. I'm fat.

Ah, just hold it in. It will. It must. It will zip up.

No, it won't. It won't, it won't! It won't zip up. I'm big, I'm fat, and that's all there is to it.

This back and forth between me and myself isn't going anywhere fast. I give up. I need new clothes that fit. A spritzy size eight until some weeks ago, I'm now a ten, maybe even a twelve. One-of-a-kind, lovely vintage clothes I've steadfastly collected over the years don't do it anymore. Exit polyester minis, little black dresses, and the tiny tops I wore in my twenties and thirties. My precious, extra-small cowboy shirts burst at frail seams, and hip-huggers I once slipped on without losing a beat won't come up above my knees. One piece at a time, I move these outfits up to the highest shelf of the closet. I can't throw them away. Not quite yet. What if I get skinny again? I delay and delay the decision to get rid of it all and start fresh.

These clothes, my history in stitches, matter to me. The very short white vinyl dress is a gift from my ex who liked to walk by my side when I wore it. The YSL high heels? I had them on the night John Kerry wasn't elected president. The demure, ankle-length, white cotton nurse uniform from the 1970s? That was my costume when I took over playing the Taylor Mead character in the remake of *Lonesome Cowboys* we shot in the Tucson desert. And then, the T-shirts bought at concerts I attended over the past thirty years, with logos of bands that mattered enough at some point that I wore the cotton memorabilia that connected me, their fan, with the musicians I admired. These shirts are markers of my slowly evolving musical allegiances to communities of Johnny Cash lovers or Talking Heads heads. A good number of the shirts, though, had been given to me by musicians I knew. Bob Log III, Al Foul, Amor Belhom Duo, The Inspector Cluzo. Me and my sunny-side tits visibly pledged fealty for many years to the bands whose logos we heralded. I flew their flags. The rest of the shirts were thrift-store finds in more or less thinned-out threads. Ramones, Joy Division, Aerosmith, whatever cheap shirt with a good name could be dug out from inside the deep bins of Value Village, St Vincent de Paul, Salvation Army. Twenty dollars could get you a lot of good shirtage in pre-eBay Tucson. But I'm in Paris now, twenty years later. How long do I hang on to these shredded bits? If I put on my much-worn, bare-threaded, pre-Calexico Giant Sand T, I look like a fast-grown child and I don't feel sexy at all. Or feel anything, really.

★ ★ ★

I cried just a little bit when I left Tucson, a couple tears at most, far from a full, heartfelt sob. The shuttle van taking me from Tucson to the Phoenix airport pulled out of the gas station parking lot on Sixth Avenue. I settled in my seat and Cat was inside her soft case carrier in the hauled trailer behind us. The suitcases jingling around her in the dark, she must have been hysterical with fear. I hadn't told the driver that I was traveling with an animal. When the van pulled up, and the door to the trailer opened, I discreetly slipped the carrier in following my suitcase and quickly walked away. The van departed and, two blocks into our trip, crossed Fourth Avenue. Quasi-deserted at this early hour, still littered from the festive evening, Fourth—as we knew it—had awakened just in time to bear witness to my slipping out, like a lover sensing the bed empty, hearing the front door cautiously shut. With one last glance back at Fourth, I saw the clubs where I had spent so many of my evenings over twenty years. The Avenue was one of the major arteries of my Tucson body, and I had loved and laughed, stumbled and stared there, growing up from style-less teen to "rose girl," the one and only certified-French rose peddler in Tucson, to local rock star of sorts.

The van crossed Fourth, Fifth, and Sixth and got onto the freeway to Phoenix. I had choked back a couple of tears, and that was it. I didn't feel much. Not even relief. Too exhausted and in shock that this was really happening. At the next passenger pickup stop on the outskirts of town, when the driver, aware at last that an animal was being carried with the suitcases, threatened to disembark Cat, it took all my strength to fight him back. This was a matter of emergency. I pleaded and invoked my imminent international flight and narrated the tale of my escape from the States. There was no leaving Cat behind. The driver was unmoved, steeling up in the way some in America can shut down empathy when asked to go against regulations. I had to make the driver understand. A story, I had to tell him a story. I was human, he was human. Palermo. I was moving to Palermo. I named the city where Cat and I would be finding refuge and, miracle, grace, at last, the driver and I saw each other clearly. An Italian driver. Yes, he was Sicilian—well, at least, his grandparents. Yes, they were from Palermo. "Of course, of course," he said, "I'll take your cat, but don't say anything to anyone, and don't report me. Now make sure her carrier is well secured. We don't want her crushed between two heavy suitcases." I slipped back onto my seat, relieved and drained, and I didn't cry anymore on the whole trip, and not for months. Two tears for Tucson, that was it. It was a close call, but I had managed to escape.

★ ★ ★

I peek through the curtain of the dressing room. "Yes, please, could you get me the next size up? Yes, same pair, same color, same everything, one size up."

Failure? Fat? This morning, I hush-hushed the inner voices that round-robin the eternal equation between size and worth, and on a burst of optimism, quietly slipped out of the apartment. Shopping day, I do declare. Feeling mighty grown-up for taking the matter in hand, and for once, for the first time maybe, acting on the very real premise that I've grown large, I hit the department stores with renewed energy.

Galeries Lafayette. They're an upmarket affair. The first store of that name, on rue Lafayette, had opened in late nineteenth-century Paris. Since then, Galeries had rhizomed across the world, from the Trump towers in New York—an unsuccessful venture, it closed after three years—to Dubai where the lobby ATM dispenses gold coin currency. But the first Galeries store I remember visiting as a kid was in Pau, the capital of my mother's home province, laying less than ten miles from the farm where she was born and grew up. In the 1960s, when she was in her late teens, Galeries Lafayette must have seemed to her like the apex of Parisian chic, the one store where you'd be tickled to spend your money. It was an aspirational, all-encompassing boutique, carrying everything from clothes to kitchenware. For those who lived in rural villages where items of necessity were usually bought from a traveling salesman making his rounds—the one who came to my grandparents' farm drove a gray Peugeot van with a back-door hatch that he flung up to reveal a cavern of no-frills essentials—Galeries must have seemed palatial.

It's noon already, and I have spent a couple hours in this Galeries Lafayette, the brand's flagship store in Paris. I've gone up and down elevators, wandered the floors in search of just the right clothes. The choice is dizzying. Why did I choose this one store and not Printemps, a block down the avenue and just as fancy and huge, or gone to some little boutique in Pigalle? Simple. I need my mother to pay. It's her store credit card I'm using. She had handed it to me last year when she realized I'd be in Paris for a while and didn't have much money coming in. That was sweet of her. I could buy anything I needed at the local food supermarket, a Monoprix. The irony of being given this unrestricted access to a food supermarket by my mother was not lost on me. I used the card in the worst way possible, turning it against myself. Unwilling and unable to refuse her gift, I made it hurt me. Maybe with clothes, I oddly reasoned, it would be different.

Silk and sweet cottons—soft fabrics—a cloth is a cloth is a cloth with a little something extra like a feel and a color, sensual harbingers of the comfort of a possession all mine, a beautiful belonging that I can make into a shell, a wanted home. It's not the first time I get help from my mother but I always ask—and get—in circuitous ways. Yes, it's with her credit card that I have reupholstered myself today, just as it was with her money that I had gone to my first Tucson shrink twelve years prior. My first face-to-face request for help had been met with scorn. She scorned shrinks, told me off angrily. There was fear in her words, and deep unhappiness. I see it now. Why else would she react so vehemently at the thought of her daughter consulting a shrink? What would be unearthed and where did that leave her, the mother? Would she be found guilty? Missing in her responsibilities? Defective and, maybe even more importantly, unhappy herself in the empty nest my parents were then renting near the Arc de Triomphe in Paris. Oh, money didn't buy her happiness but I was going to get mine with her money and let her know damage control was overdue.

I come out of the megastore to a stampede of Chinese tourists splintered on the sidewalk next to deckered buses. The winter wind is obscene; it slips into my crotch and scratches my neck. I angrily knife it back but I almost hit a bicyclist instead. Time to get out of this tight spot. The hot air gulfing out of the stores reeks of rancid adrenaline. These entertainment destinations, giant stores like mega fun castles à la Disneyworld, are horrendous to exit but I escape, brushing past and through bodies waiting and texting in lines that go nowhere fast. A whole lot of us are willingly parsing ourselves through an experience of mammoth proportions, losing sight of why and what ride we want, just waiting to crank out a card. Christmas freaking lights in November. The air is thick with torturous sugar. Is it still high luxury if it's actually purchasable? If I can see it and touch it, I don't want it on me. I want it on a wall. I never liked Disneyland. I'm afraid of elevators. I just bought my new clothes in an air-conditioned nightmare cathedral of consumption, with my parents' money and with still deep hatred of the body they were to clothe. But for now, it all fits.

I called her and explained I had bought pants and a coat, shoes—such an incredible pair, with a cat face design—and a silk nightgown. I was especially happy to have gotten the nightgown, something she never would wear at any time in her life, a sexy, soft, revealing item. Fuck you, mom, I'm a sexual being. How is that scary? Of course, my father was never privy to such solutions, our private little deals. He liked to deal out his love and acceptance in more concrete terms. Clothes were of no interest to him. *Patrimoine*, as he called it, was more essential, the transmission of his hard-earned money to his children in equal parts, the inheritance. Feelings were not part of the deal. We had to assume there were any at all.

28

THE TWO OF US are dining out in an upscale Madrid restaurant. With walls of bare white stone dotted with dimmed spotlights, the room is hushed and the guests spaced afar. I order pigeon. My American friend goes for the turbot on special. We haven't seen each other in almost a year.

The tourist guidebooks are all in agreement: this is by far Madrid's very best restaurant. I lift my glass eye-level. The tabletop candles gleefully simmer through the superb Galician red. We clink our glasses, toasting our good luck, and the sharp sound gongs over the table. There's a gentle hum in the room, a comfortable noise level that suggests liveliness without enforcing it. Kudos to getting both light and sonics absolutely right. I love this place! I can't stand these joints with tiny, lousy ceiling speakers that filter out prefab songs to their crash cymbals and hi-hat hits, a glass-fiber sort of sound, deathbed-gasping mp3s, but this place isn't one of them. What a perfect meal, what swank deliciousness. Service is unpretentious, attentive. I feel pampered, unstressed, and I've decided to luxuriate in the moment—and the food—fully. I'm not paying for my food, and my friend coaxes me on. "Choose whatever you want," she says.

We have been friends—and neighbors in our downtown Tucson niche—since the 2004 presidential election, when she helped bankroll my Suffragettes' anti-Bush voter registration efforts. From my old haunts she was the only one I could expect, aside from the musicians who flew there regularly for shows, to make the trip to Europe. With the means and time to travel, she is about to spend a month in her timeshare apartment in Majorca. Her first pit stop in Europe, though? Madrid, where she has picked a five-star hotel for the weekend.

"Would you meet me there?" she had asked. Why not? Paris was still grim, gray, and wintery, and it was time to come out of my cave. I knew she'd book us a ritzy suite and I was looking forward to visiting the Prado museum. One baby step at a time, I was venturing out again into the world of restaurant meals, drinks with friends, and one-on-one conversations. The worst might have been over and Madrid was a good way to test my solidity.

When our main dishes arrive, they are presented without ostentation by a cute but down-to-earth waiter who makes it seem as if we are the ones granting him the pleasure of our enjoyment. The whole experience is divine. We are sharing a hotel room so there's no chance I can puke out this meal without being caught head-down or stink up. Fine. Go for it. Our arms swipe back and forth across the table like so many mandibles from bottles to breadbasket, swish through the cup of tiny, yellow butters, our napkins rolled out and unleashed for the evening. Thick rye, dark. Lighter rye, airier. Slices of whole wheat, chewy and soft. My friend talks about her food, compliments it, interacts with our waiter. She's on top of the moment, a very socially enabled American woman of some means, the kind of person who has taken a course in wine pairing and appreciation, maybe as preparation or result of a trip to Europe for her fiftieth birthday. Me, I don't say much, liking to feel like I don't need to say anything, that someone is doing the hard work for me and I'm not in control. Plus, I don't know much about wine pairing and I have been stubbornly using my fork in the wrong hand ever since I can remember. Bring on the bird. I'm going to like this.

I feel like the table itself is smiling. My pigeon is so tiny, so cute, biggest bone the size of a well-shorn pencil lead. The fish on my friend's plate glows like a sunken archangel. "Would you like to taste it?" she asks. I would. I do.

This, this is food. What perfection! Fish extraordinaire. Fluffed, airy, suggestive as an architectural model. Stunned, I chew, swallow, and smile. So simple, what flavor! It's the best thing I've ever tasted, I declare. I hand the fork back. She takes it and pushes her plate toward me. "Have the rest of it," she says. "I'm not hungry." Not hungry?

The night before, I had arrived late from Paris and found my friend in her hotel room, resting in bed with the Lonely Planet guide to all things Madrid. We hugged and started catching up. She'd gained five pounds, maybe six, I assessed under breath, complimenting instead a striking new haircut. She'd chosen to go all white over a very short bob. It suits her, I say. "You look ten years younger." Divorce was shaving the years off, she laughed. She was happy to see me looking rested. She noted the dark circles around my eyes had receded since we last saw each other almost a year ago. Oh, the dark circles, sure-fire signs of my sickness. I nodded in agreement but didn't take on her thinly veiled invitation to discuss my state of health. Yes, we are friends, but what does that word mean when I've never been able to come out to her about my condition. I pretended not to understand, and we kept making small conversation.

I have many friends like her that I keep at a safe distance. All my friends are kept at a safe distance. Do they know? Have they tried prying? Do they care? I wonder how many people, friends and relative strangers, my bandmates, bartenders, booking agents, dentists, publicists, neighbors, and brothers, how many have asked themselves what the hell my problem was? And if they've figured it out, were they repulsed? Did anybody laugh or make a joke of it? Is anyone like me in sickness? Again, in Madrid, I stop short of asking these questions. What does my friend know? Is she like me? Not asking, in cryptic silence, I remain a mystery to be protected at all cost.

I know she knows what my "trouble" is. We have an indiscreet friend in common who, I'm certain, has told her the truth, but we've never talked about it and, as a consequence, our friendship has always been weakened by my refusal to confide in her. Not that she hasn't tried to reach out, compassionate woman that she is. Often in our conversations, she would drop hints that her own addiction is to food, confiding in me at least a couple times that she had struggled with anorexia as a teenager. I would listen to her and just nod, unable to do more than disengage. Giving her advice would have blown my cover and exposed me to a scrutiny I refused. We spend the weekend side by side walking and shopping the Madrid streets, and we sit in cafés nibbling on half-truths and baked almonds, and there's nothing sadder than missed opportunities to recognize and help a true friend. Why am I surprised I couldn't speak to her openly? I'm my stoic parents' child. Oh, she is patient but for how long? Why wouldn't she get wary of knocking on deaf doors? It does get tiresome, this friendship where so little is revealed that matters.

"Are you sure?" I ask her. "You don't want your fish anymore?"

"Not hungry," she replies, "I had a Toblerone at the hotel before we left. And the leftover Doritos from the open bag on the night table."

I cringe. What? But this is divine food. How could she turn it down, and for a bar of middling chocolate from the duty-free shop? That's like saying you're full from sucking on a baby pacifier. The woman is trying to calorie-control her diet at this table, on this day and in this town, after she went through the trouble of getting us to this topnotch restaurant. And Toblerone wins?

I admonish her kindly. "Really? You sure?" What a pathetic choice.

She relents, agreeing that she's being silly and takes a few more bites to appease me. Girl, there are more calories in a squirt of your boyfriend's semen than in this entire fish. Don't swallow next time, okay?

I didn't really say that to her—it didn't even cross my mind then—but it's the truth. These days, food and sex are locked in two very separate compartments of my brain. It wasn't always the case. I used to look forward to tasting the meaty hormone mashup of flavors and smell that is semen. Sex felt better on an empty stomach and I never had my cake in bed. Did I ever rub chocolate sauce over my body for a lover to lick? I can't remember if I ever did or if it's something I heard from a sweet-toothed friend. When we were still together and after I had opened up to him about my sickness, I asked my husband if he wanted to go through it with me. We would eat and eat until bursting, then puke. I thought it would be the only way he could understand me. I wanted him to know what it felt like. He refused.

★ ★ ★

The next morning, I wake to shouts and drumming beats from outside our window. I go to the balcony and look down to see a procession of hooded men carrying torches and whips. I dress hurriedly—my friend hasn't stirred awake yet—and get down to the plaza. The slow-moving parade of penitents is tailed by some Jesus look-alike bearing a heavy wooden cross. The whole thing looked more dramatic from the balcony. There's no actual bloodletting, no whips puncturing flesh. The Easter parade is all rather quaint and colorful, the self-flagellation a fake and the expiation rite toned down for the sake of skittish tourists like me. It strikes me that I might have toned down too, that my expiation rites are as demure as this PG-version of the last walk. Coming head-to-head with death, I pretend great dolor, but I'm carrying a styrofoam cross. I won't really be dying on it nor could it bear my true weight, but the crown of thorns looks good on me and it awes the crowd of onlookers to silence. Madrid is getting to me. When I return to the hotel room, my friend is taking a bubble bath. I tell her what I saw in the street but her eyes glaze over, her mind on shopping already. She is bent on getting herself some Spanish garb of the kind they don't stock at the Tucson mall where women of her age are painted beige and bland into oblivion.

Later that day, I go to the Prado museum by myself while she scouts the high-fashion boutiques. The Prado is immense. When I chance upon the *Garden of Earthly Delights* triptych, there's a crowd in front of it. I inch my way to the first row as people drop away, their curiosity satiated. I stand there, as close to the painting as I can, blind to the bodies heaving around me, for half an hour detailing the painting's panels. I balance on one foot then the other. I sense people behind me, kids sneaking up for a brief moment as close to the panels as they are allowed, testing limits. I hear comments in several languages. I'm very impressed by the painting and think of it often throughout the rest of the trip. How alone do any of the figures that people the painting feel? Do they know each other or have they been thrown in there together as strangers in this heaven and hell? Haven't they all gone mad with music and wine, fire and fears? The last panel is home, isn't it, the land where all beings hang on to the illusion that it can't end like this, that the world isn't on fire and that we must keep pretending all is well.

⋆ ⋆ ⋆

The meal too lingers, the memory of that bite of bright white turbot still with me to this day. Did I really feel sorry for my friend that she wasn't able to enjoy that meal? Did I care how she felt? Maybe I do really prefer my eating to be a deeply private experience. Alone in the enjoyment, alone with your senses and your fears of what those senses might compel you to do. I don't know, but there are not too many feasts I recall at will for the simple pleasure they brought me, not too many meals I've simply enjoyed sharing with a friend, and certainly not many dishes I can recall with a smile years after I've ingested them. That Galician fish in Madrid? An exception, I can still taste it. Bile? I will never forget the taste of bile spit either.

29

SAVE FOR THE TRIP to Madrid and a couple of solo jaunts to Mediterranean seaside towns, I remain set in Paris through the winter months and into spring. Mornings, when I chance to glimpse it from the top of Montmartre, the Eiffel Tower is gauzed with a lingering fog. December, January, February; the nights come fast and weigh heavy, stretching into dismal mid-mornings. Winter is hard. I find myself obsessively browsing through AirBnB listings for photos of sunny locales—my online city porn—and realize that I must be missing the light of sun, and a bit of nature.

What do well-off Parisians do when the gloom of winter has turned them into depressive maniacs? What would a self-aware adult, with the time and means to take care of body and soul, choose to do in that situation? Take weekend trips to cities on the southern end of the low-cost airline routes. And so I find myself spending a January weekend in Cagliari, hopping to

Marseille in February, and Madrid in March. I undertake these trips just as much for the sun as for the feeling that I'm not unlike the people I see daily in Paris, at the studio, and in my building, that I belong with them, and will have something to share that they can understand, something benign to answer when they ask how my weekend went.

At home, my sunny plans keep me harmlessly entertained. I study maps of the city I've set my sight on, and pore over schedules of bus routes and ferries like a good little detective. Projecting forward onto those streets, I look up museums and harbors, and stroll through neighborhoods and churches one Google Street View step at a time. Cat frowns at the suitcase I've pulled out a good few days in advance of my departure and, traumatized by long-haul flights, makes herself scarce for fear I might take her on a trip too. By the time I land, I have traced over in my head all the steps I need to take to survive the weekend, from airport to hotel, single room to starred café, to museum and the sea. I will walk with confidence and steer clear of the anxieties that might cause me to eat far more than is decent.

Deep down, I do feel guilty, strangely guilty for taking these trips. And I start realizing that anything I do for my enjoyment, any activity that's meant to bring me pleasure for pleasure's sake, these things are, by essence in my twisted view of the world, a waste of time and self-respect. Where is this fear coming from, this deep-seated anxiety at living?

Sunny reprieves? There's no escaping me, not even in Cagliari. I have a hard time doing nothing and soon grow tired of having to fill my days with what qualifies as entertainment in the guides I've consulted. Once I have checked into my hotel,

I start establishing a daily routine to avoid seeing that, tired, depressed, and anomalous, I'm running on fumes. Like a cat, I circle the hotel neighborhood. I find a café I like and order at the counter, not staying longer than a couple of minutes, then come back to my room, and leave it again to get another coffee. I am afraid of what I'll do when I find myself alone in my hotel room. Museums, beach walks, churches, a pile of antic stones? I should be interested but I don't go looking for them. They're beyond my strength and although I'm not quite ready to accept that I'm not interested in architectural treasures, I'm also not ready to do nothing. I don't know anyone in this town nor have I ever taken the steps to connect with strangers through phone apps or a bar pickup. I've actually chosen to be here because I don't know anyone. So I am the off-tourist in a depressing odd-season and this town all to myself still doesn't satisfy me. Against the backdrop of Cagliari's relaxed harbor, I realize how much I'm constantly, everlastingly on edge.

★ ★ ★

Back in Paris, the other dwellers and I wring the necks of our alarm clocks every morning and go to work silently kicking and screaming. Screenlit throughout the day, we pale ants get away with not looking up at the sky lest it fall on our heads. The lack of light is driving me up the wall. Mondays turn into Fridays, a sorry trick like a card shuffle you still can't figure on the nth pass. Five to six times a week, I take yoga classes where I sit down cross-legged and retreat into my body via the exquisite minutia of a routine now ingrained in my every muscle.

The light remains gray for weeks, and it's been months since I last smiled at someone. But good spring comes to those who don't despair. I have steered clear of emergency rooms by repeating to myself like a mantra that February is the month of the mad, and I'm not mad because I know that February is maddening. The fools, they don't realize that their outbursts of self-harming are prompted by the lengthening of days, a surge in light. I was warned by my shrink, who as a young'un had worked triage, that, well before hospital records could prove it, this was how February rolled; as a silent killer.

But February passes. I have gone underground to fly below toxic fumes of cars, trucks, and the many human machines. There used to be this cocoon I spun every day and unspun every night when I unraveled into the toilet bowl. There is this cocoon I now thread every day on my mat, and as long as I spin it, I am safe.

The studio door opens, lets in people, people who turn into students. The class ends and I feel like I've been trying to start a fire with plastic flint stones. The door lets my students out and, from teacher, I turn back into "not teacher" and walk away quietly after locking the studio door. Yet, every week, more and more bodies lay down on more and more mats to wait for my instructions both spoken and tactile. My classes seem to be getting more popular and I am liking that. Me, giving of myself and receiving in return the attention and efforts of my cockeyed, cross-legged strangers, side by side wishing for happiness and the end of suffering, just as I am.

★ ★ ★

One morning, after I shut the studio door, I remain a teacher. I walk out of the courtyard and turn the corner at Bataclan onto the boulevard, still a teacher. That bit of a smile on my face, this sweetness on my tongue, those are the teacher's jewels. Back in the Paris metro, I watch strangers provoke each other in fights. I hear verbal assaults. Standing where the ground opens up to the bowels of the metro system, and a generic merry-go-round dizzies up the air while the stern newspaper, magazine, and gum kiosk spits it all out, I take it in. You, there, on the concrete slab between church and city hall, trying to pass me off some flyer for some political precept, why do you react in anger when I say no? Why, you drop that nice guy mask real fast when I deny you my attention. Like a street photographer or an actor studying faces and postures of passersby, I see the smaller things we think we hide. Shortcutting each other, looking each other down, stealing air. You there, puffing on your break, I know you pull long shifts and the few words of English you know never seem to mollify the rancid tourists who spit back in your plate the unease they've been feeling all day while traipsing the hill at being bored on holidays. I know your back hurts and you want your lungs to suffer too. Not that they wouldn't. People whose bodies are viciously under attack, bodies that viciously screech at each other, animals under the stress gun. Hunkering down, I go through this self-inflicted regimen of pain—not puking, keeping it in, dealing with it—thinking that there are a lot of people who feel that bad in their bodies every day. It makes me feel less lonely, and that I've joined the ranks of humanity.

* * *

I stand on my hands in the middle of the room and hold the pose unassisted for two, three, five seconds. Back on my feet, a discreet smile on my face, I am happy. At last, I am able to do the pose without assist. Maybe because I've stopped worrying about how I look and what image I project, I find it easier to hold balancing poses, shaky as I might still be. In Crow and Side Crow, Chaturanga, Firefly, and Warrior III, all poses that require strong core and abdominal muscles, I relax. Maybe it is that simple. Good little troopers now, my thigh muscles roll inward when I ask them to. That, I can feel now. But what does it matter? Maybe there's something growing within or around or in the vicinity of my lower belly, a deep core muscle that is the center of my balance and the new power in my stride. Powerhouse abs, anyone? It matters. I know my body, I feel my body and it feels good. These are such small victories. Such great victories.

I know a couple of things now. I know that when I extend my arms, my hips resist the stretch. That never used to be the case. I know that everyone's ligaments are reeling, as mine are, from the hard work of keeping it together. I know that when I bend down and stretch that spine, the back of my legs are stiff—I'm not perfect anymore but I'm normal—and I know who's stiff there too. My hip bones anchored to the floor, my lower back screams in pain. Yours too. I know about your back pains. I know because I'm feeling it too and I'm like you, stiff with bad habits and heartbreaks that tug at the muscles around the heart and twist the mouth. Yes, what are you supposed to do with the pain? Do you have to eradicate it? Are you supposed to stick with it? Or do you run from it? Stiff from self-abuse and dangerous intakes, I share the pain. I get it. The motivation to get rid of pain? It's there too, buried under the fear of getting better, the fear of being well, and alive. I get it now. That's why people come to yoga, why they come to my classes.

30

MARCH 8TH. SUNDAY. I wake after eight hours of a sound sleep. Last night, I stayed in. I couldn't think of a single thing that'd call me outside. No one messaged and I didn't reach out to partake in things-Saturday, like going to a show, a shower, or a Bumble app expedition. Drinking green tea and more green tea, I puttered online, monitored my sites then looked for a film to watch on YouTube and found not one but two and three classics. I dragged myself to bed around three. This morning, the plots of the two Mae West films have merged in my head with that of *Moulin Rouge*—the original version. I can only make out a single, one-plot storyline about a badass woman, played from saloon to salon by the one and only catty queen as she mutates from a madame in Gold Rush Alaska to powdered society darling in some bling neon hybrid of 1920s Manhattan and late nineteenth-century Montmartre.

Binge watching is a lot more fun than I ever expected.

Take one storyline, add another, splash a bit of zzzs and a dash of imagination. Stir slowly without distressing the characters. Leave to rest for a few hours. Contemplate in the morning.

I need a good story to wake up to. In the fictitious feature mashed up overnight in my brain through that alchemic reaction between self and good filmmaking, Mae from the West has upended her odds and flamboyantly makes her own way out of a stiff western vehicle to become the best and shiniest little wheel on the wagon of Paris society. I get out of bed feeling for a few seconds like I've truly morphed into the unflappable, the fabulous West—minus the sex jokes, and I'll always be way more demure. Evaded and elated, a smile on my face as I stir… but the feeling doesn't last.

After some months of hibernation and long, anxious, at times desperate, hours of painful self-reflection verging on catatonic rumination, who was I if not a sicko? Relapsing, I had a clear answer last night. I was and would remain a sicko. Signed, stamped, and delivered.

What the hell happened? Oh, I know. I thought I was strong. Thought I had it together. Damn, this stings my pride. Thought I had won and could do it by myself. Yes, alone, the best sort of victory. I did it my way. So stupid and so ugly. Feel that belly blowing up. The throat. Oh, I won't be able to sing tonight, tomorrow, ever. No more. Why don't I stop now, stop pretending? I'll never be a singer ever again. I'll never be anything but a freaking raccoon face.

Hang on. It's not all that bad. Stop the pity party. It had been ten weeks this time. Up from nine. Victory!

Remember how good it felt to talk to a friend. Can I call someone now for help or just a bit of conversation? To say what? Oh, I don't need to bother anyone. I wouldn't bother a friend. Cat. What do you want again? Stop bothering me. Food? Yes, I will get you some. That's what I'm here for. Least I can do. You're welcome. Gotta take care of you. You're my friend. Can't you ever fucking say thanks? Ever? Talk to me. Cat!

Like a lizard with a midget tail growth, I'd been hanging in there for weeks, not puking but empty still. Why can't I be like Mae West or anyone else but me? Sister Mae, pray for me. I'm weak and I'm empty, I need my friends and I know it, now.

31

HOW DO I BEGIN? Who can I trust with my story? In the late afternoon, I am joining an old friend at the Louxor cinema for a film and a drink. Will I be able to confide in her then, when we stand looking at the Montmartre hill from the rooftop terrace? I know it now. I have to share my secret or I'll never get better.

* * *

We met in Phoenix when I was eighteen and she twenty-one. Students both—and French—on the Arizona State University campus, our friendship took roots in a shared dream of someday making our mark in cinema. Fans of flicks by European art-core directors and American ones like Jim Jarmusch—then just starting his career—we got into the habit of ditching class to meet at the library where we would request that their *Cahiers du Cinéma* collection be brought up from the vaults, one load at a time. We would sit for hours pulling yellowed copies of the legendary magazine from the carts wheeled to our table. One day, to my shock, my friend told me flat out that I was strange. I looked at her, puzzled. Yes, she further remarked, I was unlike anyone she had ever met: I was able to communicate so much without speaking. I didn't reply. If I kept quiet long enough, stared at her, then at my magazine, then at the sky, maybe we'd slip into another dimension and write, and star, in our own private outtakes of *Stranger Than Paradise*. It didn't seem to trouble her that I made myself understood through silence. Whiling away in class, I'd contemplate how it came to be that people spoke, and what they meant, really meant, when they did. What could I have told my friend? That I was stuck in a teenage existential quagmire and embroiled in some prescient, nihilistic philosophical battle? No. More likely, I had just slipped away again into my new favorite fairytale, *Wings of Desire*, released that year, and in my head, was playing and replaying its hypnotic title track. I never told her that only a few months prior, I had been dangerously frail, an anorexic; and she never guessed what was troubling me. Neither of us had words for it at the time. Already well ensconced in the cover-up strategy that had allowed me to remain a blank screen to my friend, I was learning from my beautiful Berlin angels—Nick Cave in particular—to thicken my smoke screens and refine an aura of mystery. My friend liked stories and later developed a talent for spotting the good ones into a career. In the years since our youthful campus escapades, she had followed my reinventions, from filmmaker to lyricist to performer, as so many character developments in an epic adventure film. In opacity, our friendship had remained more or less intact to this day.

Fast-forward twenty five years. Now, my old friend and I stand on the top floor of her cinema. Rooftops beyond and a blushing sky, the sun is setting over Montmartre. We're toasting each other tonight, having had enough of a run in life to know you can only deal the cards you've been given. To a friendship that has endured.

Our trajectories seemingly opposite but in truth strikingly parallel, we had both remained loyal to our dreams of cinema. My friend however, having been early on soberly realistic about her chances of ever striking Cahiers gold as a film director, had decided to produce other people's stories. I had remained a dreamer and, at nineteen, moved to Hollywood where I was sure to become a filmmaker.

It's easy. I tell her that I'm sick. I tell her everything. I give it to her like I've never given it to anyone and it's simple, and not at all scary. Speaking up doesn't even require the sort of bravado I'd put into ordering a fried sea cucumber dish.

★ ★ ★

It had one day become evident, a revelation at the age of seventeen, that I should be making movies. A single shot did it. I was watching *A Clockwork Orange* for the first time, thinking the Arizona Surbiton that had replaced my French countryside not so wildly different in spirit to the redemption-less world of the Kubrick film. In the TV room of our family house, its chromium oxides swishing over the magnetic head of the VCR, the VHS tape was purring along when, at the sight of the very first frame of the villa rape scene, I froze. Freezing? Yes, maybe I was cold, certainly was. Already, I was eating very little and the house was equipped with A/C, a novelty for my parents who cranked up the necessary dial for our comfort. Rented movies were my time-out escape, a daily nighttime ritual, and none had more of an impact than *A Clockwork Orange*. The villa rape scene starts with a fixed wide shot with the house and its manicured lawn in the background of the frame and a name post or house number in the foreground. It's nighttime but there are lights inside the house. Nothing out of the ordinary, there's likely a nice family inside, watching TV just like I was. Jolting me as they creep in from the off-camera boundaries of the frame, the bodies of men inject themselves in the story, all sniggering giggles. I had seen something worth living for. Someone, I thought, a film director, must have had a lot of fun thinking up this visual joke, using all the elements in his complete control. As wicked Alex and his sorry henchmen tore through the frame, I knew it. I wanted this kind of fun too for myself. This was self-indulgence and pleasure of the highest order, the kind that could never be berated by my parents. This was pure decadence masquerading as hard, ambitious work and a most challenging profession. How would my parents raise any objection? It was a far cry from the baton-twirling majorette I had wanted to be when I was six. A few years later, when I was asked who I was going to be when I grew up, I would answer by asking a series of questions. What's above, hierarchically speaking, a school teacher? School director. What's above a school director? The district administrator. And next? The minister of education. And the president of the republic. Yes, that's what I wanted to be. I wanted to be president. My parents loved telling that story. I was well trained into reaching high, no matter that I was a girl. My father had done it himself with hard work and smarts, rising to safety and comfort from an impoverished childhood raised by a single mother, tragically early-widowed with a brood of five. I had to give it to him. He didn't blink an eye at my dreams as long as I did my homework, helping, in that instance, by instantly getting me several very practical books on the jobs available within the film industry and how to get them.

⋆ ⋆ ⋆

I've told her everything and my old friend is visibly moved. I am too. She reciprocates with a tale of her own, hinting at her daily ritual at the bathroom scale. Yes, she admits to watching everything she eats. I check on my own thoughts and listen to my heartbeat for a second. Was it so bad opening up to her? How badly am I shaken by the act of speaking up? Not too much. I painted broad strokes on that blank screen of mine and she heard and accepted my story, and told me so. I feel alive and safe.

32

SUNDAY IS ALWAYS A pretty good day to practice outside the house. The streets are more or less quiet, the bike ride somewhat less hurried. Getting to the studio feels like a happy, careless stroll. Sundays, like lonesome Saturday evenings, leave me wanting for something harmless to do with myself. Yoga, the default choice, is always there to fill the void. At this point in a year of almost daily practice, I don't have to think about it. My life revolves around yoga. I'm on track, chugging along calmer than I've been in a long while, but I start to think that maybe I am faithful to this lifestyle more by momentum, fearfulness even, than true passion. What if I tried changing a bit of the routine, take a chance on a new studio? I believe I might be able to handle that much novelty, and, as I ride my bike *du jour* to a studio I've only recently joined, I laugh, picturing a snail tentatively popping out one eye, then the next, ready to suck it all in again at the slightest brush of a troubling breeze. By spring a frequent defector to my alma mater studio—I haven't taken a class with the boss in weeks, although still under the influence of his style—I was becoming responsible for my own path. Amazed that it took me so long to realize it, I had been stagnating in classes whose sequences I could follow eyes and ears closed.

Flying through République on my bike, I veer left toward canal St. Martin and ride up to Parmentier. This "other," competing studio advertises Mysore and Ashtanga classes, both styles of yoga I've never tried before. There's also an intriguing community class on Sunday mornings. That's what I'm here for. Community. I'm still looking for it in Paris, my community.

I'm at the front desk checking in with the magnificently-limbed teacher, string-bean lean and flippantly supple, an outed ballerina in yoga spandex. I pay ten euros—this class is donation-based—a bargain, when the front door slams open behind me. Fresh air swirls through the stuffy lobby, sticky with sweat and reeking from the acrid deeds of morning classes. A woman, stomping her way to the desk with a bright pink yoga mat, lands on the desk, breathing loudly at my side. I look at her sideways, annoyed by her disruption. I want peace right now, an incense-soaked bath of soothing grunts, relaxing poses alongside like-minded bodies. And silence, which the woman has broken. Has she been racing to get to class on time? Shoo, shoo, lady. What's this commotion all about?

I know too well that, in a city this size, getting to class on time can be unnerving. Factor in the Ubuesque stop-and-starts on the metro trains, topped by aboveground traffic jams and, most days, most students, having already sprinted through to make it, then take a half-hour on the mat to unwind. I know I do. If I want to maintain some sort of stress-free lifestyle, then I have to plan my days around class schedules. Is this where my life begins shrinking? Is going to yoga classes now my one and top priority, along with living unstressed and unharmed? As a teacher, serenity helps. After all, I am there to offer reassurance to my students that the class they are paying for will help them feel better.

With two elbows on the counter, the panting woman, who should be thrilled she's made it to class on time, is complaining about having to pay for it. Discreetly, I stay near the desk so I can hear her out, a bit of a perverse move on my part and a teacher's reflex. Do I want to convince myself I am above that state of stress and, in essence, am superior to the unfocused, ungrateful woman? I'm always fast in judging harshly my own motivations. Couldn't it just be a protective instinct toward the teacher? From one to the other, I know what she is now having to deal with. Tricky customers happen and we are of the service industry. But no matter my motivations for hovering at the desk, I understand at last that the unhappy student is in possession of a ten classes pass, technically good for any classes in the studio except… this one. The teacher explains. "Well, it's our weekly community class. You give what you want, with a minimum of five euros."

The woman balks. "No, I've paid already. No one told me. I've just spent an hour and a half on the metro to get here. I will not pay five more euros to take a class I've paid for already."

Frustration mounting, the woman storms back out. I picture her radiating hatred at every step of her way back home through the city. Like a nasty cold bug spreading from one face to the next, her anger latches on to every single person she finds herself near. Oh, city dwellers. The teacher sighs, and we look at each other. There's not much else to say. I go set up my mat in the room and sit, eyes closed, wishing for some peace of mind and waiting for the first Om, and the first pose.

Not much else to say? There is actually, and it is being said over and over in my head during class. This woman who walked away? I didn't lift a finger to keep her here with us. Why? I remained calm. Brownie points for that. Good girl. It's true that the situation didn't escalate into a shouting match. The woman wasn't mean but she was annoying, and unappealing. She stood out sharply in contrast to all that the studio promoted. Peace and universal love. Okay, she was looking for a bargain. She needed a bargain maybe, needed a break from her day. We failed her. I failed her.

Yoga is action. I heard that phrase a lot during training but didn't give it much thought. Yes, it is, of course. It seems self-evident that yoga is an activity, a physical activity even, as opposed to a motionless contemplation, but if I can't really define what yoga is, then maybe I can start by defining what action is and, as a result, get to some deeper understanding of yoga.

I let that woman walk away. She was getting on my nerves and her strung-out rant ribbed me. But now that she is gone and I have not helped her, I feel terrible and very imperfect as a yogini. Here I am, butt up in the air, vulnerable and somewhat looking ridiculous in a lovely headstand that cost hours of my life and thousands of euros to perfect, and I think this has all been a joke. Today, I was given a chance to act, to help someone feel better. Did I? Yoga is action, *prof* kept hammering at us. Did we get it? Action. Why didn't I think of just plopping a ten euros bill to pay for the woman's class? Or even a five? Oh, basic human skills, where art thou? It's a bitch being a decent person. There are no days off, no Sundays ever, from compassion.

33

SIVASANA, THE RESTING POSE. Also called the Corpse pose. She is lying on her mat, arms tight alongside her skinny body. Two little mounds, the hip bones, are poking through her sweatpants. The cheeks are hollow and the eyes sunk deep into their sockets of blue and black flesh.

One more minute and I'll rise the class up from corpse, get everyone out of the door and go home. I could use a coffee and some lunch. I look at the girl again, still as a dead body on her mat. I know her trouble. Should I talk to her after class? What could I say? Should I do something? And how? This ain't pretty. If she breathes, nothing moves, not a ripple. I wonder what is coursing through her veins at this time. Can't be glucose. She doesn't strike me as a cookie monster. More like a cookie-hater. Might be she lives off eating angel dust of the sort ground from paper wings. I wish I could talk to her and tell her she's got the spelling all wrong. It's not A N O R E X I A. It's a four-letter word and it's spelled H E L L. Tell her that she doesn't even realize how bad she's got it now and that she's one breath away from failure of the heart.

I'm failing her if I don't speak out. No. I can't say anything to her. I shouldn't. What could I tell her that she'd be able to hear? I know she sees me—and us all—as monsters, fat monsters, repulsive and alien, we of average weight and normal appetites. Should I slap her then? Hit her? Maybe I could just yell at her, spook her? I'm afraid she might collapse, though. I cringe to think someone—a friend, a doctor, a mom if she's lucky—told her that a yoga class would help her. She's not twenty, although her looks might be deceiving. She seems older but I could be wrong. She has no age. I can't teach someone like her. Yes, I will slap her. And yell.

I do nothing of the sort. Instead, during class, I place the palm of my hand gently on her lower back and softly say to her, "Breathe in. Now, out." In. Out. A human touch is priceless in cases like hers. She is trying, I can tell. I know she is listening but I also know it's not reaching her. She's swallowed the key to her own house. Whatever she does with her body at this instant, whatever she does with herself is not reaching her. She's lost consciousness. No, I don't mean she's knocked unconscious on the mat. On the contrary, she is paying a lot of attention to the class, like a good, attentive, and dutiful little student. In other words, she's got a one-track mind and a thin-as-a-rail body and the two don't talk. Freaking anorexic. Wake the fuck up. That shit ain't funny long. Please, do something!

She'll be back and I'll keep placing my fingers on her lower back, on her shoulder, and, in doing so, try to wake her up to her own body. Do not hurt her. Maybe someday she'll remember that touch and understand what it was meant—without words— to tell her.

★ ★ ★

A year ago, when my journey as a teacher began, I learned a very specific Vinyasa routine and practiced it with regularity of intention. I learned the sequence by heart and eventually was able to teach it just as I had been taught, its exact pacing assimilated, experienced, and enjoyed. Engaged in the act of transmission, I was aiming to be nothing more and nothing less than a happy cog in the wheel. There was peace in that.

Slowly however, over months of teaching, I begin adding my own personal touches to the sequences. I find myself slowing down the pace of my classes and spending more than just a few breaths in the same pose. One student remarked I was going for depth. Maybe, I replied, I was just exploring the cave, thoroughly sweeping every cobweb in the room before exiting to the next, as I did when I prepared the room for class, sweeping and tidying every corner. Over the course of the winter, as my body slows, weighted and exhausted by the rapid changes I am subjecting it to by allowing myself to eat and keep the food I ate, I allow myself to spend more and more time in restorative poses, the kinds that are held for long minutes of stillness. I then share these poses with my students by incorporating one, then two, in the hour class.

By summer, a year after my certification, when the time comes for the studio to draft a new schedule for the fall, I get offered a better slot on Wednesday mornings. I ask if I can make it a yin class. In yin practice, the poses are held for up to five, seven minutes, sometimes longer. Experimenting at home, I would overdo them at times and hurt myself by staying put for fifteen or twenty minutes. Always one to go for pain, I had learned to manage my body and to take the time off needed to heal sore ligaments and an overstretched spine. My more vigorous Vinyasa classes have slowed down too. I get to correct and assess, leading students to be introspective about the way they practice. I don't want them to be mechanical, to lead them in an aerobic routine. I want them to question what I do and what they do, and eventually why they do it. It seems more important.

I come across *Some Rules for Students and Teachers* by educator and artist Sister Corita Kent, via John Cage. "Number three: First duty of teachers is to get everything they can out of their students." But that's only half the story. Corita/Cage also rules that the "first duty of students is to get everything they can out of their teachers." A good yoga teacher will lead you to stillness within movement through a steadiness of intention and with a voice that inspires confidence and letting go. If the performance is right—and teaching is a performance—a teacher will invite you into the eye of the storm. Yes, it is the students' responsibility to keep it worthwhile for the teacher to battle the rising gale. As on a stage, when I feel myself helping the audience help me so that, together, we can make good music, so in the yoga studio, I live for these rare, precious times when, together as people, we breathe new life into old poses and old tunes.

"Don't be taught. Teach yourself." This is what I thought I

should have said to my students after the class ended. I should have said, "Dear ones, we're gathered here today to make you lose your balance and to partake of instability and practice not poses but thought. Forget your abs and your pecs. No, you'll not be doing in my class what you came to expect from other classes at this studio. I will slow down and take apart the routine, then slow it down even more. You will be forced to sit with yourself and within your bodies, and to sit in silence as if meditating. Because I want to frustrate your expectations and I want you to deal with it. I know. You want this pose to follow that pose. Your body knows the way and leads the way? Don't let it.

"This is not an exact science. We will mess up and make mistakes. Accept it. But don't expect me to spoon-feed you a series of movements that you can follow on automatic pilot. I'm here to turn off that pilot. Practice not being bothered by uncertainty. No matter what I say and no matter what I ask you to do, your breath is your raft, your guide, and your conscience. And if you think of, if you breathe into where you throw your leg, and how you hold your foot, you will not get hurt. It's all a dream. Keep it that way."

34

PARIS. ANOTHER SUNDAY LATER in the spring. I'm not going to yoga today. I need something else. What do I do then? What would a cat do?

The May sun says, Come on outside and walk alongside me. Already the day feels like the start of something else, a different life, simpler and more beautiful—if for no other reason than I slept well and the sun is shining when Cat climbs on the bed and wakes me. Cat and me, we've been close this past year. In a couple of weeks, it will be my birthday. Will I again spend it pacing through an airport, at last on my way to make Palermo home? Where will I be running to this time? Haven't I had enough of running? I shrug aside the question and get dressed.

All day again, Cat will stay inside. I still don't like it. Poor thing. Why did I think it a good idea to bring Cat to Paris? Before I go, I open the glass doors to the balcony and retrieve a half-dozen mousy toys from behind the couch and under the sink. Wouldn't it be better if she lived somewhere else, I ask myself, a place with blood and bones critters? She won't be entertained long by her bouncy balls. When I return, I'll dig them back again from dusty corners.

I go out and spend the day wandering the streets. I head east from my street and walk a half hour, past two train stations toward the canals. Along the water, the air is crisp and nudges me onward. Summer is stirring. I stand by a small pedestrian bridge. There are people near, sitting on benches or on the ledges of the canal banks. There are couples and there are those who look to couple. The city has prettied up, trees with fuller hems and greased leaves. I am walking hand in hand with the sun. Ain't it sweet, I think, to be kissed by the sun.

I head north. The streets empty out. It's not postcard-pretty Paris around here. There are no longer any tourists. I don't linger. I hear my breath as I walk, and walk keeping my spine straight, my lower back curved, my shoulder blades tucked in and spacious, in yoga-styled perfection. Watching every single step I take, I am a walking machine, a precision of movement. I bounce, my body breathing by and of itself. I am a breathing being, a thinking machine.

★ ★ ★

Inside the Space Shuttle of my dream, their safety belts unbuckled now, the astronauts know. They know now this is the end. I watch them as they get up from their seats. They take a step toward each other and they hug, holding each other through their contraptions of metal and flesh. Without words or tears, without any trace of grandiloquence, in the simple and sober way that people can acknowledge one another, they are saying goodbye with an embrace, a tight, warm, and very American hug. In a few seconds—an eternity—a minute at most, the capsule will have exploded from the enormous outside pressure and the force of a logic beyond and of itself magnificent. They know it, and knowing it, all of them, one by one, choose to do this—a farewell hug—with the little time they have left. They could be screaming or praying, still in their seats, but they choose instead to act, and win, in the name of love, in that capsule shooting fast down through our very precious atmosphere. I wake up smiling. It was a good dream. Now, I know what I didn't know back in 1986 sitting through a minute of silence in that Arizona classroom. These strangers around me were my friends, the shuttle and its American dream were going down fast, and, through thick and thin, we were in this all together.

★ ★ ★

At the end of the long, radiant afternoon, I walk by the Anvers Square in Montmartre, then through the outdoor market whose stalls line up along its eastern edge. The merchants carry fruits and vegetables, produce that is colorful and full of life in the mild late daylight. I gorge on the beauty of shapes and colors, purple potatoes, delicately green fennels. It's a sensual pleasure, a breath of air. I buy strawberries and eat them from the box walking through the market. I rejoice in silence, not making waves, content with myself and my small victories. Nothing is simple, especially not food for me. My quiet victory lap around the stalls feels hard won, but I leave the market relieved. Happy? Ecstatic with strawberries.

From the Anvers Square, I walk toward the Goutte d'Or neighborhood. On my right on boulevard Rochechouart stands the Louxor cinema where I performed months ago now. To think this is the street corner where, only a year ago, I would bitterly have ridden over anyone who stood in my path on the way to training. Where has my anger gone, the distrust and self-hatred? I don't mean anyone harm today, not even the hellcat who almost runs over me and two other pedestrians from her bike lane. May the dragon she-rider slow down before getting killed or maiming anyone on the downhill path to République. Standing under the papyrus columns of the Louxor facade, I look up from the metal scarab marquee grid to the top floor. How easy it had been on that terrace, I remember, to open up to a friend about my bulimia. In turn, she had confided in me and we've been doting on each other since with renewed curiosity, filling in one glass of wine at a time the black holes in our life stories. I envy her ability to have kept steady and even in her choices when I became a yoyo queen, bouncing from one identity to the next to survive changes in continent, language, and professions. Slender and tall still, she has changed little from her ambitious and curious twenty-one-year-old self. This same control over food, people, and phobias is certainly the key to her professional success. Is this who I should model my eating patterns after? Do I want her life and successes? What's wrong with my life and successes? Nothing, nothing at all.

I pass through the Bashung Park in Goutte d'Or and find

myself on the eastern end of rue Ordener, the large, leafy street leading up to my parents' place. I know why I wandered here. There is a mural I like seeing. It changes often. On Sundays, graffiti artists, kids, parents bring their spray paints and a pack of sodas. They paint and repaint. They erase and complete. It's an ongoing project. Today, I walk by and watch them color the wall. Getting closer to it, I see at one of its extremities a small stencil I've not noticed before. It has been sprayed close to the bottom of the wall, black letters over a red background. *Bien trop de femmes dans bien trop de pays parlent la même langue. Le silence.* "Way too many women in way too many countries speak the same language. Silence." It strikes me as true. To be and remain silent? No more. I will speak up. I am a woman. Not a cat. I am one of many. I am not alone.

35

DURING ONE YEAR OF wrestling with my recovery, teaching in Paris on sabbatical leave from the stage, I had recorded my progress by taking daily notes on both my yoga and meditation practices. Some days, I would log just a couple of words—"feast, no dreams"—or I might make a note of the number of students, nameless always, and exult at their prowess and mine on the mat. I also kept tally on my puking habits. This was what mattered most. From the start, I knew the end result of my journaling would be this book, my junk memoirs. I would be observing and recording myself without judgment, an attitude that is the basis of the yoga that had been transmitted to me in Tucson and Paris. In that, yoga had been my patient teacher, alternately hammering and whispering that, if only I kept showing up on the mat, all will be what it is.

With a year's worth of self-observation in two red notebooks, it was time to leave Paris and find a place where I would begin the work of shaping my notes into a tale I could share. Would it be Sicily, my promised land? But a year later, Palermo wasn't any longer the right place for me. I needed peace and quiet, a town where I knew no one. In Palermo, I thought, how could I steer clear of requests for interactions, and nights out meleeing on the harbor? What I needed was a small town, far from airports, isolated as an island, and where I would be and remain a complete stranger. With a budget set low for monthly rent, I hit the maps of Europe intent on avoiding cities where I had performed and might be remembered. I also crossed out countries with harsh winters, drawing over the western hemisphere a latitude line that ran through Barcelona, Rome, and Istanbul. Any small-size city south of that line would satisfy my need for sunshine, cheap rent, and privacy. Then I found it, the town for hermits and writers.

★ ★ ★

I hadn't planned on liking Basilicata so much, but, over several writing retreats starting in May 2014, I learned to love this tiny region of Southern Italy for its stubborn streak. Like yoga, Matera, its capital city, had always been there, weathering millennium after millennium with the patience of stone. From the beginning, I was certain I knew no one in Matera and that cinched it for me. The photos I had seen of the Sassi, the old town neighborhood, a stunning, many-thousand-year-old assemblage of caves and paths, houses carved into the cliffs and churches dug out from the rocks, also made Matera look wonderfully alluring. It was peaceful, close to nature—five minutes from my door, I could be hiking alone in a nature reserve—cheap, and mesmerizing. It was the perfect small town for the next step in my recovery; a new adventure—writing.

★ ★ ★

Cat couldn't know where she was headed when we left Tucson. I didn't either, really. Fleeing the States, I aimed for Palermo but ended up missing Sicily by a few hundred miles when, three years after that ill-thought-out and lugubrious stay in the old Sicilian palazzo, I made my way to Basilicata. I wouldn't bring Cat this time. For a year, Cat had softened my landing and kept it cool in Paris for me. Silent witness certainly to my trials but not immune to the detachment they created, Cat had been vital company, a link to our shared past in Tucson. Cat had seen it all but Cat was a two-way mirror. I gave Cat up. We were done. I was ready to roam again and didn't think it fair—or very practical—to put the animal through the stress of another round of uprooting and the pains of mass transportation. It'd been a little over a year from the time we got on that American Airlines flight to Europe, Cat in the bilges, me in eco class. The sight of suitcases still unsettled her.

Growing up, I didn't have pets. My parents had always refused us, and I don't remember ever pressing the issue. They had, very firmly to my child's ears, said no. Except for a short-lived, fluffy brown hamster—it died shortly after falling in our pool in Arizona, where I discovered it shivering inside the water filter nook—we never kept a dog, cat, turtle, or even a goldfish. My parents thought pets were unnecessary, an "extra" that wasn't worth the trouble, in the same way that they still believe that baths are a waste of time and water. Could pets for companionship and emotional comfort also be just plain fun? No, they were a waste of money. Life could very well be lived—and had to be endured—without furry emotional crutches. Did I believe, like my mother, that a dog was meant to look after a herd of cows and a cat was only useful as much as it hunted the many mice that would have devastated stored grains and animal feed? No. I wasn't brought up on a farm. My mother was. I wasn't brought up struggling in a small town like my father. My maternal great-uncle would regularly beat his dog when it failed to run after and control his cows. My grandmother would enlist my help to locate the new kittens their mother had birthed somewhere on the farm, maybe in the hangar stacked to the ceiling with a maze of rectangular hay bales. After I had reported on my findings, proud of the success of my detective work, grandmother, retrieving the kittens from their litter, would take them to a bucket of water she had prepared and—population control, no more, no less in her eyes but in mine, a betrayal—dunk the little ones to drown.

Even now, my parents, retired and settled in a country house with a yard big enough for half-dozen tigers, felt no need for the company of an animal. It seemed odd, improbable to imagine them caressing Cat, enjoying it. Hoping, praying they'd warm up to her and would find it in themselves to give her the love—and brushes—she needed on a daily basis, I pretended to drop Cat off for just a few weeks, but what I really wanted was for her to work her charms and be adopted for good. My mother, to whom, before this day, I would have cringed at entrusting anything that not just belonged but meant the world to me, would now be taking care of my Cat, I hoped. Yes, I had grown up a bit. Yes, it was possible to let go, to allow my mother in without fear of her eating me alive. Such was, I had always felt, the power she had over my life. I could not have imagined it happening but I'm letting go. To me symbolic of a newfound freedom, this handing over of the animal would mark a new period in my life. I would stand alone, strong and free of fears. I was ready.

★ ★ ★

Finally, in winter 2015, I stop teaching. It's been a year and a half since training, a year and a half of continuous growth as a yogini, a growth only teaching could allow. No longer a rookie at the studio, I graduated to well-attended midweek slots and taught Yin. The classes proved popular and I enjoyed teaching them. Their format was not mandated from above, and I was able to incorporate information I had gleaned during my travels to Berlin and the States from Yin, Pilates, and Intelligent Movement teachers whose methods were unorthodox by the standards of my Paris studio. But I give away my slots, upgraded by then to three mid-morning ones. Someone else, a newbie from the latest crop of trainees, is now getting up before dawn to teach the 7:00am classes which used to be my lot. I need time. I want to go back to making music and to performing.

A couple of months later, I stop going to the studio but

keep practicing daily on my own at home. Once in a while, a friend realizes I used to teach and asks that we do some yoga together. I say yes the first few times, happy to share what I know and spend time with a friend, but soon I learn to deflect the requests. I have become very particular about what I do on my mat, forgoing set sequences altogether and making up my own, somewhat unorthodox ways. Untrained friends are rarely able to follow my train of thought without getting sore, or worse, getting injured.

* * *

In 2016, however, I briefly go back to teaching during the month I spend in Calais. I am volunteering in the large warehouse that supplies food, clothing, and shelter to the thousands of migrants. At the end of a first shift moving boxes in the cold across concrete floors, I realize how backbreaking the work is and witness the level of stress that afflicts the long-term volunteers, some of them months into their commitment. I can help, I decide. I know how to bring a bit of wellbeing to tensed bodies. After asking for donations of mats from my alma-mater studio in Paris, I return to Calais and set up nightly classes in a conference room of the Calais youth hostel bordering the sea. The classes are free. By 7:00am, after work, the volunteers are glad to relax and roll around on the floor. There's not much else I can provide. I'm not skilled at very much that's useful at the warehouse—not carpentry nor cooking—but I learn to sort through boxes of boots, loafers, high-heeled pumps and jelly shoes donated from England and France, looking for the elusive and prized black sneakers in size 43 to 46. Evenings, I teach a handful of students. It is only the beginning of 2016 when I am in Calais. The experience leaves me disorientated, somber, and sobered-up. By fall, I am all of these things still when we return to the camp with donations gathered each night after the shows of my first German tour since moving back to Europe. A week later, October 2016, the Jungle camp is being razed and migrants dispersed.

★ ★ ★

That winter, my father lands in the hospital with a cancerous appendix and something switches in the dynamics of our family. My parents are getting older, and we three children have to figure out among ourselves how to deal with new responsibilities and visiting hours. He can't eat much solid food for a few dreadful weeks. I visit him one afternoon, early on in his recovery. He's weak and has lost some weight. A tube needles calories from a drip bag into his veins Another plastic tube sucks out stomach acid into a pouch placed on the floor at his bedside. The content of that pouch is brown bile and stomach fluids. I know that color. I've felt that texture. I would even be able to recognize its smell if it wasn't sanitarily contained in the pouch. This is puke bile from an empty stomach: the bitter, biting one. I tasted it often.

Of course, I think, Dad would get hit there, in the appendix where things get stuck and rot. Anger, fears, ruminations and dreads, the unspoken, depression, self-doubt… they all live there in that hole in the core of a body, a dark star full of the pain that colors an entire life and becomes the one and only reality. I know. I've been there, in that black hole.

Mother is putting on a good face and a good fight, as always the little foot soldier for the family. She shows up at the hospital every single day, entering the room as soon as the morning routine check-ups have ended and leaving past sundown. I look at my father on his hospital sickbed. His blue sanitary gown is pulled up high over his thighs. Is it odd that his penis rests between his legs for anyone to see? Growing up, I remember times when he'd get out of bed and walk around the house with a morning stiffy. Maybe here too, in this hospital room, the display means he is comfortable in his own skin. A more likely explanation? Belly flattened by the lack of solid food, my father is lying on his bed with dry lips and an uncharacteristically unfurrowed forehead. Anti-anxiety pills make him look twenty years younger. Damn, these pills, they do a better job than Botox at erasing deep wrinkles—and how they work wonders to inhibit self-consciousness. Come close to death—some get there by accident, others by comeuppance—flirt with it if that's more your thing—choose your weapon, the options are many—and maybe, if you're lucky, you will make it out lighter, enlightened maybe, and it won't matter that your skin is hanging. Oh, no, it won't.

I look at the pouch full of bile, and blurt out "Hey… whoa!" But I stop myself. No. I can't say that. Not here. Not now. Not ever. I can't go on laughing awkwardly in my father's hospital bedroom and speak these words, "Hey… I know what it is. That's bile in the pouch. Funny. I know just what that tastes like," showing off my hard-earned knowledge about nature and the human body. Wisely, I remain silent. There might well be poetic justice in this pouch of bile but no matter how much I need to connect the dots and make sense of my own story, this is not about me. I shut up.

36

STILL, ON RARE OCCASIONS, I throw up. Once every few months, when, wound up from a tour or a visit to my family, I get back to whatever is "home" at the time. Whenever I haven't found a way to shut out the world and carve some time to relax.

When the binging and puking happen, I don't beat myself over it. I pick myself up, make a cup of ginger tea and think calmly about why I did what I did, and what other wonderful things I could have done instead of acid-bathing my front teeth with green goo. On nights when I can't come up with any of these wonderful things, I now know to label this lack of inspiration as depression and simply go to bed. The next morning, I put on my big glasses and, hidden behind the dark pink-shaded lenses I've become notorious for, go face the world one task at a time.

* * *

In late 2016, with the money from the sale of my house in Tucson, I buy a wooden sailboat moored in southeastern England. Me, the desert cat who thrived on dry rivers, summer monsoon storms, and flash floods, I now live on the Kent Riviera onboard a 42-foot mahogany, oak, pine and teak ketch that, if I ever learn to sail her, will one day—let me dream—take me across the ocean to America. I move onboard, and days, then weeks and months, a whole year, pass and I keep well. I forget that binging was ever an option. I forget what puking feels like. This is still going on. I have found a home, and I love.

* * *

Today, I'm sanding and varnishing the beautiful teak on my ketch. I'm reading the online papers, feeling sick in my stomach at the news from the States. I email my representatives in the U.S. Congress and, since I am in England now, put up a Vote Labour poster on my deck. I'll be doing yoga later, a combination of poses my body is screaming for after I've spent the morning immobile writing these lines on the computer. I know what I need from yoga and I get it with a little effort. Tomorrow, I'll get on a plane at London Heathrow and fly over to Tucson for rehearsals with my new bandmates, young women from my old town. We're playing shows in Germany again in a month, May 2017, a very reasonable mini-tour of six dates—even my touring has become more relaxed these days, if not entirely stress-free.

★ ★ ★

I stopped meditating after I realized that failing to comply with the self-imposed obligation of a regular daily practice was stressing me. With one less thing to worry about, I have struck a manageable balance between anxiety and contentment. I'm far from a perfect yogini and far from a perfect paragon of health but, at one with my flaws and my rotting teeth, I've slackened up on controlling my body. It is, I accept, a collection of twitches and undulating waves of pain and pleasure, here now, gone shortly afterward. I try to hold on to neither pain nor pleasure. I am the most normal person in the world, as adjusted or maladjusted as anyone I know, but you won't hear it from me. Not yet. I may have written these lines but you won't be reading them until I've been free from bulimia for many, many months. Only then, when the time is right and I'm someone else at last, will I trust not to break from the offering.

★ ★ ★

Because I've gone into my lungs and found them breathless, because I've gone into my heart and found it empty, because I've opened my hands and found them speechless, I feel stronger now. I also feel lighter. I've made some choices and given up on things I loved. I gave up on living in Tucson and I put aside performing for over a year. I stayed put and let it hurt. Like a recovering alcoholic, I'll always live with the raging child inside me but I'm not a slave to it any longer. I eat very fast—devour—when alone, on tours, and in stressful situations. I'm not interested in fancy dishes or much variety in my meals. When I share food with a friend, I eat slowly and enjoy our time together. I watch my weight and still obsess at times about the right and wrong food to eat. I haven't turned into an alcoholic and still don't use any drugs. As adjusted or maladjusted as any of my friends, I have wasted more food in twenty years of bulimia than would fit inside this boat of mine. I have misused more resources than should have been made available to me. I am an American, deep down a monster in an atrocious land.

The boat is rocking gently. I am watching the news and feel nauseated, yet I still love an imperfect world. I can't help it. It's beyond myself. I am beyond myself.

ACKNOWLEDGEMENTS

For their invaluable assistance, kindness and generosity, I am indebted to

Gérard Arnaud, Megan Amber Cox, Dr. Patrice Mathieu, Dr. Louis Teulières, and Olivier Régin.

John Parish, Mitch Cullin, Andrew Smith, David Jennings, Shaun Hendry, Megan Garrett-Jones, and Raphael Mann.

Carole Scotta, Anne Argouse, The Inspector Cluzo, Richard Siken, Lela Campitelli, Michelle Ascoli, Allyson Ezell, Anne Presting, Paul Wallfisch, Luigi Di Pace, Tiziana Schillaci, Marcella Di Palo, Jon Jost, Keja Ho Kramer, Ann Scott, Maura Pell, Brendan Kelly, Joshua Karp, Annie Dolan, Connor Gallaher, Brittany Katter, Vicki Brown, Jim Waters, Yan Péchin, Sergio Mendoza, Marco Rosano, Thøger Lund, Chris Rush, Jacinta Elliott, Gerard Elson, Pamela Sutherland, Joe Mabbott, Hannah Levin, Naïm Amor, Lauren Garlovsky, Al Foul, Lucas Moseley, Emmanuel Plane, Luc Rollin Goodhart, Ulrike Presting, PJ Casey, Mike, Andrew and the Archive crew.

Jamie Keenan, Francesca Baker, Flavien Prioreau, Cynthia Karalla, Stéphane Macquaire, Greg McNamee, Fiona Hallowell, Anne Horowitz, Scott Pack, Reg Walker, Andrew Lownie, Elizabeth Jennings, Ricardo Fayet, Nathalie Bru, Andreas Loizou, Nicholas Reece, Alex and Sara Ratcliff, Ellie Jones, Lara Clifton, and David Gaughran.

Bastien Forestier Rischard, Frank Jude Boccio, Ashley Leal, Humberto Pena Sanjurjo, Filipe Gomes, Antonia Courcier, Renee Raiteri, Arthur Vint, Sophie Burch, Tom Santo, Thomas

Bohnet, Bryan Lurie, Cynthia Elliott, Tom Prezelski, Julianne Pharris-Berger, Juliana Murphy, Kristina Janni Ståhl, Aaron Chatterson, Uta Bretsch, Tino Tuch, Bill Carter, Norbert Lutz, Xavier Cadet, Terry Edwards, Casey Golden, Daniel Zanzara, Nocky Noke, Laura Linden, Klaus Kynast, Pierre de Gaillande, Chris Wagganer, Guuz Hoogaerts, Stephen Guardigli, Jonathan Kugel, Rebekah Le Magny, Nicholas Gray, Antonio Bras, Carole Chiaramoni, Gudrun Thäter, Alenka Pavlin, Léo Spiritof, Stefan Mitsopoulos, Rachel King, Brett Wilmore, Catherine Watine, Brad Holland, Ani Cordero, Oliver Gray, Susan Gallaher, Judith Edge, Deirdre Saravia, Anne-Sophie Terrillon, Phillip Woolever, Laurent Bocahut, Simon Davis, Luz Elena Mendoza, Kay Massmann, Pauline Jansen Van Rensburg, James Andrews, Rennie Sparks, Frank Blass, Molly Simon, Michael McMurchie, Eva Umbauer, Peri Pakroo, Jeana Hadley, Graham Beard, Michael Dinsmore, Alex Kaliwoda, Joachim Walter, Adrian Schwarz, Susan Haynes, Sammy Decoster, Bill Bragin, Fabienne Bouvil, Ingrid Irene Downey, Katie Haverly, Sylvain Ansoux, John Mount, Beatrix Wood, Enid Pifeteau, Linda Ray, Pierre-Yves Linot, Callie Snyder, Gilles Calfort, Eric and Jane Force, Ed Spillane, Georg Cizek-Graf, Tom Fox, Volker Schneider, Olivier Conan, Kaitlyn ni Donovan, Barbara Letellier, Loïc Mahé, Julie Jennings Patterson, Dietmar Leibecke, Achim Spyra, Thomas Belhom, Cathy Viale, Henry Rosenthal, Stefania Arnesano, S. Lynn Wright, Danielle De Picciotto, Rich and Susan Hanson, Stephan Frucht, Carole Chiaramoni, Miranda Schubert, Astrid Serafini, Sadie Hennessy, Steve Jillings, Claire Dugué, Jessica Hardy, Gudrun Thäter, Charlie Anson, Charles de Lint, Steve Curran, Cyril Moya, Norbert Jäger, and Fabrizio Cammarata.

Defne, Ece, Georges, Jean-Michel, Lamia, Laurent, Lubna, Marie-France Dissard, and Marie Maubarthe.